Discrimination and the Law

Malcolm Sargeant

Routledge
Taylor & Francis Group

LONDON AND NEW YORK

First published 2013
by Routledge
2 Park Square, Milton Park, Abingdon, Oxon OX14 4RN

Simultaneously published in the USA and Canada
by Routledge
711 Third Avenue, New York, NY 10017

Routledge is an imprint of the Taylor & Francis Group, an informa business

British Library Cataloguing in Publication Data
A catalogue record for this book is available from the British Library

Library of Congress Cataloging in Publication Data
Sargeant, Malcolm.
  Discrimination and the law / Malcolm Sargeant.
    pages cm
  ISBN 978-0-415-63195-2 (hbk)—ISBN 978-0-203- 63194-5 (pbk)
  ISBN 978-0-203-50076-7 (ebk) (print)   1. Discrimination—Law and
  legislation—Great Britain.   I. Title.
  KD4095.S26 2013
  342.4108'5—dc23
                                                        2012044524

ISBN: 978-0-415-63195-2 (hbk)
ISBN: 978-0-415-63194-5 (pbk)
ISBN: 978-0-203-50076-7 (ebk)

Typeset in Joanna
by RefineCatch Limited, Bungay, Suffolk

Printed and bound in Great Britain by
TJ International Ltd, Padstow, Cornwall

Outline Contents

Detailed Contents

Preface

This book is intended to be a broad introduction to discrimination and the law. It includes a lot of UK and EU material and is focused, although not exclusively, on discrimination in the workplace.

Like all my books I have tried to write about the law in a way that can be understood by non-law students as well as those who study law. This book has been written for students who are new to the subject and who are probably studying law, HRM, business and management, and so on.

An understanding of discrimination law is an essential piece of knowledge for many people at work and I hope that this book provides that understanding.

Malcolm Sargeant

Tables

Glossary of Acronyms

BAME	Black, Asian and Minority Ethnic
BIS	Department for Business, Innovation and Skills
CJEU	Court of Justice of the European Union
DDA	Disability Discrimination Act 1995
DWP	Department for Work and Pensions
EAT	Employment Appeal Tribunal
ECJ	European Court of Justice
EHRC	Equality and Human Rights Commission
EIRO	European Foundation for the Improvement of Living and Working Conditions
EPA	Equal Pay Act 1970
ERA	Employment Rights Act 1996
ET	Employment Tribunal
EU	European Union
FTSE	Financial Times and the London Stock Exchange
IRLR	Industrial Relations Law Reports
LGB(T)	Lesbian, gay, bisexual (and transgender)
MPL	Maternity and Parental Leave etc. Regulations 1999
MSHW	Management of Health and Safety at Work Regulations 1999
NEET	Not in employment, education or training
ODI	Office for Disability Issues
OECD	Organisation for Economic Co-operation and Development
OHS	Occupational Health and Safety
RRA	Race Relations Act 1976
SDA	Sex Discrimination Act 1975
TEU	Treaty on European Union
TFEU	Treaty on the Functioning of the European Union
TFR	total fertility rate
UNDHR	United Nations Declaration of Human Rights

Table of Cases

Table of Legislation

Chapter 1

Equality

Chapter Contents

1.1 Purpose

The purpose of this chapter is to introduce the concept of equality and to help define what is meant by the term. We will also discuss some of the causes of inequality and look at some evidence that discrimination on the basis of unfounded stereotypes continues to exist. The important but often neglected subject of multiple discrimination will also be considered. This is where someone is subject to discrimination based upon a number of personal characteristics or, indeed, a combination of those characteristics.

1.2 How fair is Britain?

The Commission for Equality and Human Rights produced a triennial review on inequality (2011c), which stated that:[1]

> Between 1995–97 and 2006–08, a steady growth in the number of jobs raised the percentage of women and of Black people of working-age in employment by twice the average, and the percentage of Bangladeshi and Pakistani people of working-age in employment by three times the average.[1] However, some groups with low employment rates have done badly over the long term, especially those pushed to the margins of the labour market. For example the employment rate for disabled men without qualifications halved between the mid-1970s and early 2000s. Calls to the Equality and Human Rights Commission's helpline also indicate that employment issues are significant for disabled people with over half of the calls in 2008–09 related to employment issues coming from this group.[2]
>
> Despite some growth in their employment rates, only 1 in 4 Muslim women work, and many face practical barriers preventing them from doing so. Moreover, Black people and disabled people in their early 20s are twice as likely not to be in employment, education or training (NEET) as White people and non-disabled people. Young Muslims are also more likely than Christians to spend periods out of the labour market. Overall, a more demanding job market is less forgiving of those without qualifications.
>
> Many barriers within employment are breaking down, for example with a growing proportion of managerial and professional positions taken by women. However, the British labour market continues to be characterised by a high level of occupational segregation. Around 25 per cent of Pakistani men are primarily taxi drivers; women make up 83 per cent of people employed in personal services; and over 40 per cent of women compared to 15 per cent of men are employed in the public sector, making women particularly vulnerable to public sector cuts.
>
> Occupational segregation continues to feed pay differences, especially in the private and voluntary sectors where at age 40 men are earning on average 27 per cent more than women. The large proportion of women in part-time jobs also contributes to this. Occupational segregation also explains differences in illness and injury rates in the workplace, with people in manual and routine occupations being most at risk.

1 Hills, J. *et al*. 2010. *An Anatomy of Economic Inequality in the UK*. Report of the National Equality Panel. London: Government Equalities Office. Tables 10.3 and 10.4.
2 Calls received by the Equality and Human Rights Commission's helpline 2008–09.

---

1 Reproduced with the permission of the Equality and Human Rights Commission (EHRC).

There are few large-scale data on the labour market experiences of lesbian, gay and bisexual (LGB) people. However, we do know that LGB adults are around twice as likely to report experiencing unfair treatment, discrimination, bullying or harassment at work than other employees. This is also mirrored in the nature of the queries received by the Equality and Human Rights Commission's helpline, many of which relate to harassment in the workplace suffered by this group. There are even less data available for transgender people, though smaller-scale studies point towards evidence of harassment and other forms of discrimination in the workplace.

The report also states that surveys show that we are more tolerant of difference and less tolerant of discrimination nowadays, but it also reports that what happens in the real world still falls short of the ideals of equality, such as 'the harassment of disabled people, to homophobic bullying in schools, to stereotypes and arbitrary barriers that prevent older people from giving of their best in the workplace'.[2]

Undoubtedly we have progressed a lot from the days when women had to give up work when they became pregnant or when accommodation owners were able to refuse applications for tenancies from people because of their nationality or the colour of their skin. The above extract from the Commission's report gives some idea of the challenges that still remain if we are to achieve equality.

1.3 Equality

What do we mean by equality? Do we believe that that all people should be treated equally, or that only similar people are treated equally? Should the principle purpose of equality legislation be concerned with achieving equality of opportunity for everyone or should we be more concerned with achieving equality of outcomes? These are really important questions and the way in which we answer them will influence the sort of protection from discrimination that is extended to people.

As an illustration we can look at a hypothetical factory that has a production line predominantly staffed by female employees. The heavier jobs such as driving forklift trucks and lifting and carrying bulk items tend to be done by male employees. The 'white collar' part of the operation has mostly men in management positions and women doing admin/secretarial work. This not an uncommon situation, but what is wrong with it, if anything? All the shop floor staff are paid similar rates, although there is extra pay for those doing heavier work. The management and secretarial/admin staff are on a job-evaluated grade structure and their pay is related to their performance in their jobs. All the shop floor staff are treated equally; all the management and admin staff are also treated equally.

The problem is that in such organisations women have traditionally occupied the lower paid jobs and men have occupied the management jobs, and this is still the reality in many of them. If we take the most senior jobs in organisations, namely the members of the board of directors, we can see the results of a long history of gender inequality. A review carried out by the Department for Business, called *Women on Boards* (BIS 2011), found that in 2010 women made up only 12.5 per cent of the members of the corporate boards of FTSE 100 companies. The review quoted research by the Equality and Human Rights Commission, which stated that, at the current rate of change, it will take over 70 years to achieve gender-balanced boardrooms in the UK.

In our hypothetical factory it is not enough that shop floor workers are treated equally. We need to ask why the heavier jobs are mainly done by men. Is it because men are stronger than women

---

2   See Chapter 1 of the EHRC report: *How Fair is Britain? Equality, Human Rights and Good Relations in 2010.*

and can therefore do heavier jobs, which are often better paid? Such a view relies upon a stereotype of men and women, namely that men are stronger and women are weaker. This is obviously not true. Not all men are stronger than all women; some women are stronger than some men. Yet having this stereotypical view encourages the employment of men in the heavier and better paid jobs, which in turn perpetuates the inequalities in pay and promotion opportunities.

One further situation in the hypothetical factory that we might consider is that of a person with a disability. Let us assume that the employer has an equal opportunities policy that includes automatically giving applicants with a disability a place on a recruitment shortlist, providing the candidate has the relevant qualifications and so on. This is a policy adopted by many employers in order to overcome some of the obstacles that people with disabilities have to face when applying for jobs. In this hypothetical situation the applicant has arthritis and is applying for a job that requires good keyboard skills. At the interview it emerges that the arthritis is in her hands and makes it impossible for her to use a keyboard. The employer reluctantly turns her down on the assumption that there are no adaptations that they can make which would enable this candidate to do the required job. Has the applicant suffered discrimination based upon her disability?

The answer to this depends upon what we mean by equality. The person has been turned down because the employer believed that, regardless of what aids were available, she would not be able to do the job of keyboard operator. This is the only reason that she failed to get the job. This might seem very reasonable, and may be the position in which some employers have found themselves. On the other hand one should ask the question as to why the candidate has been turned down. The answer is that she failed to get the job because she had a disability. As will be seen in Chapter 5 on disability, the employee may well have a case to argue that she has been treated in a way that amounts to disability discrimination.

These illustrations are intended to show that the issue of what is meant by equality and discrimination is not a simple one. Are we interested in formal equality or a more substantive approach? The principle of formal equality requires the equal treatment of equal cases, so it does not take into account any material differences between those being compared. In this approach discrimination against men is as bad as discrimination against women and there is no difference in the approach to the two groups. It does, however, ignore the fact that women are much more discriminated against than men. This approach is reflected in the legal definition of direct discrimination. The principle of substantive equality takes into account the material differences between individuals or groups. This approach might be said to try to achieve de facto equality and thus will attempt to take into account the reality of the position of women, rather than to apply some universal standard: for example, women are much more likely to have a caring role in the family and a substantive approach to equality will take this into account.

The formal equality approach might allow bad treatment of individuals or groups as long as everyone is treated equally badly; a substantive equality approach might try to correct the wrong. The case of *Glasgow City Council v Zafar*[3] concerned Mr Zafar, who was a United Kingdom citizen of Asian origin. In the case at the House of Lords it was recorded that he was employed for some ten years by the Strathclyde Regional Council as a social worker. He was dismissed in March 1989, the reason for his dismissal being given as sexual harassment of clients of the Social Welfare Department of the local authority and of fellow employees. The House of Lords considered the issue of 'less favourable treatment' (Chapter 3 explains that this is the definition of direct discrimination) on racial grounds. The original tribunal had concluded that an inference of less favourable treatment could be drawn because, as the tribunal stated,[4] 'to treat someone in a way which falls far below the standards of the reasonable employer gives rise to a presumption that that person has been treated

---

3 *Glasgow City Council v Zafar* [1998] IRLR 36.
4 Reported in the House of Lords case; see note 5.

in a way different from the way in which others have been, or would be, treated'. Thus there was a presumption that bad treatment could be inferred to be less favourable treatment by the standards of a reasonable employer. The House of Lords stated that this was wrong and that one could not rely upon the idea of a reasonable employer treating everyone fairly. The House stated:

> The alleged discriminator may or may not be a reasonable employer. If he is not a reasonable employer he might well have treated another employee in just the same unsatisfactory way as he treated the complainant in which case he would not have treated the complainant 'less favourably' for the purposes of the Act of 1976. The fact that, for the purposes of the law of unfair dismissal, an employer has acted unreasonably casts no light whatsoever on the question whether he has treated the employee 'less favourably' for the purposes of the Act of 1976.

Thus it is possible for an employer to be a bad employer and treat everyone badly. In such circumstances it may not be possible to show discrimination because nobody is treated less favourably than anyone else.

Another way of discussing these issues is to ask the question whether it is desirable to pursue equality of outcomes rather than equality of opportunities. Equality of opportunities means removing barriers to disadvantaged groups, but it also means that we must take a positive approach to ensuring that disadvantages are compensated for. It means that, effectively, everyone starts from the same point, so a person with disabilities has those disabilities compensated for in order to bring that person to the same starting point as another without the disability. Equality of outcomes is something more controversial because it means levelling out the finishing point as well as the starting point. Equality of outcomes is a process where one tries to achieve the desired result of more equality by active interventionism. Thus a quota system for women on the boards of public companies to make sure that there are as many women as men on such boards would be a way of achieving such equality. The problem with this approach, and perhaps the problem that makes it most controversial, is that it may achieve some form of equality only by discriminating against those not in the protected group. Therefore, having more women on the board may stop some men from being board members.

There are no easy solutions and this is reflected in the fact that the UK's anti-discrimination system is a mixture of policies aimed at achieving formal and substantive equality on a number of grounds.

1.4 Stereotyping

An equality approach might require individuals to be treated on an individual merit basis rather than on some other basis. The problem with a merit-based approach, of course, is that it can be subjective rather than objective, and is likely to be measured against the conventional norms of society, which tend to be those of the dominant group – white males. An equality approach requires that individuals are treated on an individual basis rather than on the group basis of a stereotypical approach.

It has been suggested that the word 'stereotype' was first used in the eighteenth century to describe a printing process whose purpose was to duplicate pages of type. The usage of the word later developed from the idea of producing further images from a stereotype into reproducing 'a standardised image or conception of a type of person' (Collins Dictionary). The problem with producing this 'standard image', or stereotyping, is that individuals are treated as members of a group, rather than being treated as individuals. It is the group to whom we attribute generalised characteristics, which clearly cannot possibly be the characteristics of every individual within that group.

One simple assumption, as illustrated in our previous example, might be that men are stronger than women. The result of this is that only men might be considered for physically demanding jobs, which, in turn, may be the higher paid jobs in certain types of employment. The outcome is that women are discriminated against in the selection process and end up earning less than men.

Another example might be the stereotypical attitudes that employers have towards the abilities of employees based upon their age. In one survey of 500 companies a question was asked about at what age someone would be too old to be employed. Of the respondents 12% considered people too old at 40, 25% considered them too old at 50, 43% considered them too old at 55 and 60% felt they were too old at 60.[5] The relationship of these judgements to conventional stereotypical attitudes can be shown in their answers to questions about agreeing or not agreeing with statements. Figures such as the 36% who thought that older workers were more cautious, the 40% who thought that they could not adapt to new technology and the 38% who thought that they would dislike taking orders from younger workers suggest that stereotypical attitudes remain strong. Research indicates that there is little evidence that chronological age is a good predictor of performance.

1.5 Does discrimination still take place?

The answer to this is yes. A Eurobarometer survey that took place throughout the EU[6] found that discrimination is widespread throughout the European Community. When citizens in the EU25 were asked about whether discrimination was widespread or rare, their response showed that many believed it was widespread (see Table 1.1).

These figures record only the perceptions of individuals and are averages from across the EU. The survey report suggests that there are widespread differences between different Member States, but that generally the view is that being disabled, being a Roma, being older, belonging to an ethnic minority or being homosexual tends to be a disadvantage in their country. This is reflected in a further analysis provided by the Eurobarometer survey (see Table 1.2).

There is no reason to assume that the situation is any different in the UK, although it is fair to say that the situation has improved over the years. Despite this improvement, inequalities do remain and obvious ones include the continuing gender pay gap for all employees, which is still a little under 20%; and the employment rate for people with disabilities is just 50% compared to about 79% for the non-disabled population.

People appear to think that it is a disadvantage to be disabled, a Roma or an older person in our societies. This is further confirmed by the respondents' assessment of which people are more or less likely to get a job, be accepted for training or be promoted (see Table 1.3).

Table 1.1 Discrimination in the EU

Ground	Rare (%)	Widespread (%)	DK[7] (%)
Ethnic origin	30	64	6
Disability	42	53	6
Sexual orientation	41	50	9
Age	48	46	7
Religion or beliefs	47	44	8
Gender	53	40	8

---

5 These percentages are cumulative.
6 European Commission 2007.
7 Don't know.

Table 1.2 Is belonging to one of these groups an advantage, or a disadvantage or neither, in society at the current time?

Characteristic	Disadvantage	Neither	Advantage
Being disabled	79	15	–
Being a Roma	77	15	–
Being aged over 50	69	24	–
Being of a different ethnic origin	62	30	–
Being homosexual	54	39	–
Being part of a different religion	39	54	–
Being a woman	33	54	1
Being aged under 25	20	38	39
Being a man	4	45	49

Table 1.3 Would you say that, with equivalent qualifications or diplomas, the following people would be less likely, as likely or more likely than others to get a job, be accepted for training or be promoted?

	EU25 (%)		
	Less likely	As likely	More likely
A person aged over 50 compared with a person aged under 50	78	16	4
A disabled person compared with an able-bodied person	77	16	4
A person who is not White compared to a White person	59	32	4
A person of different ethnic origin than the rest of the population	58	32	4
A foreigner compared to a national	58	31	6
A woman compared with a man	47	45	5
A homosexual person compared with a heterosexual person	45	44	3
A person who practises a different religion than that of the rest of the country	32	58	3
A person aged under 25 compared with a person aged over 25	30	43	23

Thus the perception is that older people will find it more difficult to get work, and the same is true of people with a disability.

1.6 The grounds for discrimination

A limitation of the statutory protection from discrimination in the UK and the EU is that it relates to a closed number of grounds of discrimination. In the Equality Act 2010 these grounds are referred to as 'protected characteristics'. There are nine of these protected characteristics, which are listed in section 4 of the Act. They are age, disability, gender reassignment, marriage and civil partnership, pregnancy and maternity, race, religion or belief, sex and sexual orientation. Below we describe the limitations with regard to multiple discrimination (i.e. discrimination based upon more than one ground), but it must be true that discrimination takes place on other grounds also and one debate is whether we should have a longer list of protected characteristics or whether the list should be open-ended. An example of this can be seen in Article 14 of the European Convention on Human Rights. This states that:

> The enjoyment of the rights and freedoms set forth in this Convention shall be secured without discrimination on any ground such as sex, race, colour, language, religion, political or other opinion, national or social origin, association with a national minority, property, birth or other status.

This, of course, has a number of grounds that are not included in the Equality Act 2010, such as political opinion (although this might in some ways be protected by the protection for belief), property and birth, but it is the last three words that contrast most: namely 'or other status'. This suggests that the list contained in Article 14 is not a closed list and that it might be possible to develop other grounds for discrimination claims.

What other grounds might one wish to be included if there were to be a longer list? The Equality Act 2010 contains a provision for the possibility of adopting the protected characteristic of caste as a tenth ground of protection (see Chapter 3). There are potentially many others, such as socio-economic status where poorer people may suffer disadvantage because of their economic position; or 'postcode' discrimination where stereotypical views can be found about people according to where they live; or discrimination on the basis of appearance. There seems to be some evidence that fat people suffer from prejudice perhaps because of the characteristics that are stereotypically associated with obesity.[8] The list is potentially a long one.

An alternative approach that has been suggested is to unite around one general principle of, say, human dignity and to use this broad concept rather than using a series of individual grounds. There is then, of course, a problem of defining what is meant by this broad concept of dignity. The idea has been around for a long time and was in the United Nations Declaration of Human Rights (UNDHR),[9] often regarded as the pillar of many measures around the world that protect people from discrimination. Indeed, the Convention is mentioned as justification in the preambles to the EU Equality Directives. Article 1 of the UNDHR states that:

> All human beings are born free and equal in dignity and rights. They are endowed with reason and conscience and should act towards one another in a spirit of brotherhood.

It has to be said that there is no satisfactory answer to the problem of definition of dignity. The courts in Canada have considered this in a number of cases, and in one case[10] the Supreme Court held that:

> Human dignity means that an individual or group feels self-respect and self-worth. It is concerned with physical and psychological integrity and empowerment . . . Human dignity is harmed when individuals and groups are marginalized, ignored, or devalued, and is enhanced when laws recognize the full place of all individuals and groups within Canadian society.

---

8 See O'Brien et al. 2012.
9 Adopted in 1948.
10 Law v Canada (Minister of Employment and Immigration) [1999] 1 SCR 497.

1.7 Multiple discrimination

One of the issues that would be resolved by adopting an approach such as the one based on dignity would be the difficulty that people currently have in making multiple discrimination claims. The Equality Act 2010 (see Chapter 3) provides, in section 4, that there are nine protected characteristics. These are age, disability, gender reassignment, marriage and civil partnership, pregnancy and maternity, race, religion or belief, sex and sexual orientation. Section 9(5) also provides that caste may be added as an aspect of race at some time in the future. These are the 'grounds' on which one can make a complaint of direct discrimination,[11] indirect discrimination,[12] harassment[13] and victimisation.[14] The problem with this approach is that it is difficult to bring a complaint on the basis of a number of protected characteristics. It may need separate complaints if one wishes to bring a complaint based upon two or more protected characteristics. Sometimes this is not possible because the two or more protected characteristics combine to create a new one. A simple example is that of a black woman who wishes to complain on the grounds that she has suffered discrimination because she is a black woman, not only because she is black or only because she is a woman. It may be the combination of the two that has caused the discrimination. She has no remedy in law except to complain about race discrimination or sex discrimination. Everybody has more than one protected characteristic, even if these are only age and sex. Most of us have a sex and we all have an age, but it is not possible to complain about being discriminated against because one is an older woman or a young man. Yet the reality is that both happen, for example the complaints from older women TV presenters about discrimination on the grounds of age and sex at the BBC. Many people have several protected characteristics such as an older (age) black (race) Christian (religion) woman (sex) and so on. Bringing cases based on the combination of characteristics is not straightforward. Despite this, there have been a number of cases where there have been multiple issues at stake.

One such case was that of *Ministry of Defence v Debique*.[15] Miss Debique was a serving soldier and a single parent who made a complaint of indirect race and sex discrimination against the British Army. She had to make two separate complaints of course, one under the Race Relations Act 1976 and one under the Sex Discrimination Act 1975. She lived in St Vincent and the Grenadines when she was recruited by the Army at the age of 19. As a result she moved to the UK and served both in the UK and in Germany. She subsequently became pregnant and gave birth to a daughter. Initially she left the child with family in St Vincent but subsequently brought the child to the UK when she was 12 months old. Miss Debique then experienced a number of problems associated with childcare and being a serving soldier in the army. The issues were related to the requirement that she be available 24/7 for her job and the immigration rules that stopped her bringing a family member to the UK to look after her child when she was on duty. What was particularly interesting was the way in which the employment tribunal combined the two complaints. It was the combination of the 24/7 requirement and the immigration restriction that put her at a disadvantage. The tribunal found, first, that women were at a disadvantage compared to men because they were more likely to be single parents, and this disadvantage was caused by the combination of the need to be always available to work and the restriction on bringing her sister to the UK to help with childcare. If either one of these issues had been relaxed, then the whole problem would have gone away. If the 24/7 requirement were relaxed, then there would not be a childcare issue, just as if the immigration rules were relaxed, there would also not be a childcare issue. When the case was appealed to the Employment Appeal Tribunal (EAT), the court stated that:

---

11 Section 13(1).
12 Section 19(1); excluding pregnancy and maternity, which are dealt with elsewhere.
13 Section 26(1)–(3); in relation to age; disability; gender reassignment; race; religion or belief; sex and sexual orientation.
14 Section 27(1).
15 [2010] IRLR 471.

> In general, the nature of discrimination is such that it cannot always be sensibly compartmentalised into discrete categories. Whilst some complainants will raise issues relating to only one or other of the prohibited grounds, attempts to view others as raising only one form of discrimination for consideration will result in an inadequate understanding and assessment of the complainant's true disadvantage. Discrimination is often a multi-faceted experience. The Claimant in this case considered that the particular disadvantage to which she was subject arose both because she was a 24/7 female soldier with a child and because she was a woman of Vincentian national origin, for whom childcare assistance from a live-in Vincentian relative was not permitted. The Tribunal recognised that this, double disadvantage reflected the factual reality of her situation.

Thus the court accepted the reality of this combined discrimination, despite the fact that the complaints had to be brought under two separate pieces of legislation.

1.7.1 Combined discrimination: dual characteristics

The Equality Act 2010 introduced, in a limited way, protection from direct discrimination on multiple grounds, although the government has decided not to bring it into effect. Multiple discrimination occurs when a person is discriminated against on more than one of the protected characteristics. The Act limits this to two characteristics. Thus section 14(1) states that:

> a person (A) discriminates against another (B) if, because of a combination of two relevant characteristics, A treats B less favourably than A treats or would treat another person who does not share either of those characteristics.

A complainant would need to show that there was less favourable treatment in relation to the combination of the two characteristics. The relevant characteristics that could have been combined in this way are age, disability, gender reassignment, race, religion or belief, sex and sexual orientation (section 14(2)). An example from the Guidance is:

> A black woman has been passed over for promotion to work on reception because her employer thinks that black women do not perform well in customer service roles. Because the employer can point to a white woman of equivalent qualifications and experience who has been appointed to the role as well as a black man of equivalent qualifications and experience, the woman may need to be able to compare her treatment because of her sex and race combined to show that she has been treated less favourably because of her employer's prejudice against black women.

1.7.2 Additive and intersectional discrimination

Two types of multiple discrimination that have been suggested[16] are 'additive discrimination' and 'intersectional discrimination'. The first consists of a situation where the person complaining of discrimination belongs to two separate groups, both of which are affected by discrimination legislation, for example a lesbian woman or a disabled black man. This is where a person may be able to justify individual claims under different statutes and they are essentially additive in nature. The second type consists of intersectional discrimination where the multiple discrimination cannot usefully or effectively be broken down into its component parts. It is where the sum of the parts is something more than the constituent elements. Thus a young black woman may suffer

---

16 See, for example, Hannett 2003.

discrimination in a way that an older black woman does not. The grounds for complaint should be that she is young and black and a woman, not necessarily three different complaints under, first, age regulations, then racial discrimination and then sex discrimination. Intersectional discrimination is where the different forms of discrimination meet but result in a form of discrimination that is not covered by any of the individual statutes or regulations. An example of this is occurred in *Burton v De Vere Hotels*.[17] Two young Afro-Caribbean women were amongst the casual staff waiting at tables during a dinner attended by 400 men. There was an after-dinner speaker, described as a 'blue comedian', who was a guest at the dinner. During his after-dinner performance the two waitresses were clearing the tables. When the speaker spotted them, he made sexually and racially offensive remarks. The two waitresses brought a complaint against the hotel that employed them under the Race Relations Act 1976. They complained that they had been unlawfully discriminated against on the grounds of their race by their employers. The reason that this unpleasant experience is related here is that these two waitresses were actually picked on because they were young, black and female, yet they brought a claim only for racial discrimination. In a different legal system, which recognised intersectional discrimination, they perhaps should have been able to bring a complaint of being discriminated against because they were young black women and not just because they were black.

1.8 Discrimination outside employment

It is worth bearing in mind that, although the focus of this book is on discrimination that takes place in the work environment, it also take place elsewhere. Examples of this include the treatment of older people in the health care system where some 65 per cent of patients admitted to hospital are older than 65 years and some 70 per cent of beds are occupied by this age group. Many of these patients are frail and, according to a report funded by the King's Fund (Cornwell et al. 2012), their experience of hospital 'can determine the direction their life takes thereafter'. The report summary states that:

> There is evidence of discrimination against older people in hospital. Age-based discrimination has almost disappeared from NHS policy since the 2001 *National Service Framework for Older People* (Department of Health 2001),[18] but it has not gone from practice (Lievesley *et al* 2009). In response to survey questions, older people tend to complain less and be less critical than younger people (Lievesley *et al* 2009).[19] Even so, they are less likely than patients in younger groups to describe their care as 'excellent' and more likely to say that they felt 'talked over as though they were not there' (Care Quality Commission 2011b).[20] There is evidence of ageism among all staff; regrettably the evidence is stronger for doctors than for other professional groups (Lievesley *et al* 2009). Older people have differential access to services: they wait longer than younger people in A&E departments; are less likely to be referred to intensive care or to have surgery following trauma; have less access to palliative care than younger people with cancer; and are investigated and treated less than younger patients for a range of conditions including cancer, heart disease and stroke.

17 [1996] IRLR 596 The decision in this case was held, by the House of Lords, to have been wrongly decided in *MacDonald v Advocate General for Scotland; Pearce v Governing Body of Mayfield School* [2001] IRLR 669; the facts of *Burton v Devere* are used here for illustrative purposes.
18 Department of Health (2001) *National Service Framework for Older People* (2001) London: Department of Health.
19 Lievesley, N., Hayes, R., Jones, K. and Clark, A. (2009) *Ageism and Age Discrimination in Secondary Health Care in the United Kingdom: A Review from the Literature*. London: Centre for Policy on Ageing.
20 Care Quality Commission (2011) *National NHS Patient Survey Programme. Survey of Adult Inpatients 2010. Full national results with historical comparisons*.

This is quite shocking because it means that the majority group of patients are treated much less well in hospital than younger patients.

The NHS is tackling age discrimination, but the issues to be faced include:

(i)   low overall rates of provision of those interventions which are relatively more important to older people – for example, hip and knee replacement, cataract surgery, occupational therapy and chiropody;

(ii) low relative rates of access of older people to specialist services compared with younger people or refusal of particular treatments or care;

(iii) low referral rates to particular services;

(iv) unthinking and insensitive treatment from individual members of staff.[21]

Another example of discrimination outside employment is that of Martin Hall and Steven Preddy,[22] who were refused accommodation in a small Cornwall hotel because of their sexuality. Mr Hall and Mr Preddy were a same sex couple in a civil partnership (see Chapter 7). The hotel was owned and run by a couple of devout Christians who believed that sexual relations should only take place within the bonds of marriage between a man and a woman and so refused to accommodate them. Mr Hall and Mr Preddy subsequently made a successful complaint of discrimination on the grounds of their sexual orientation.

1.9 Summary

Irrational discrimination based on stereotypical images of individuals and groups continues in the UK and elsewhere. There is plenty of evidence to show this, although clearly this has changed over the past decades and it is interesting to speculate about what role the law has played in changing attitudes.

This chapter has introduced the idea of equality and what is really meant by it. The view that one adopts will influence the way in which the equality legislation is regarded and the extent to which exceptions should be made. Is the aim of equality legislation to treat all equally or should there be a much more substantial approach that uses the law not only to make discrimination unlawful, but also to help achieve equality. This latter approach may mean adopting some positive discrimination measures in favour of underrepresented or discriminated-against groups and individuals.

Multiple discrimination is a reality for many people, but the law only permits complaints upon individual protected characteristics. As a result some people may not have a claim for discrimination, or may not be able to pursue the correct claim, because of the law. There are problems associated with adopting measures allowing intersectional claims, such as who would be a suitable comparator, but is that a reason for not taking action against this form of discrimination?

---

21 Department of Health 2002. This extract is found on p. 19 of the Report.
22 Case No 9BS02095 between MARTIN HALL and STEVEN PREDDY Claimants and PETER BULL and HAZEL MARY BULL Defendants.

Chapter 2

European Perspectives

Chapter Contents

2.1 The European Union

The EU has a long tradition of tackling sex discrimination and working for equal pay between men and women, although its legislative enactments on discrimination in relation to other grounds of discrimination, including race, are much more recent.

The original treaty establishing the European Economic Community, signed in Rome in March 1957, contained Article 119, which committed each Member State to the principle of 'equal remuneration for the same work as between male and female workers'. This was undoubtedly a far-reaching principle to have adopted in the 1950s, although the motivation may have been more commercially based than rooted in any human rights agenda. If one country had a policy of equal pay for men and women, then that might put that country at a competitive disadvantage compared to another country that did not have such a policy.

The principle of non-discrimination is a fundamental principle in European Community law. This was recognised as early as the 1970s when, in *Defrenne*, the Court of Justice stated that 'Fundamental personal human rights form part of the general principles of Community law, the observance of which the court has a duty to ensure'.[1] This case concerned the struggle of a female Belgian airline steward against a rule that enforced her retirement at the age of 40 years. This recognition of equality as a fundamental Community right has enabled the Court of Justice to interpret Community and national legislation in a positive way, rather than just using a narrow interpretation of the text. An example of this can be seen in *P v S*,[2] which concerned the dismissal of a male who informed the employer that he was to undergo gender reassignment to transition to a woman. The case was about whether the prohibition of sex discrimination, contained in the Equal Treatment Directive, also applied to this transgender situation. The Court stated that:

> the directive is simply the expression, in the relevant field, of the principle of equality, which is one of the fundamental principles of Community law.

It also stated that:

> the right not to be discriminated against on grounds of sex is one of the fundamental human rights whose observance the Court has a duty to ensure.

In a strong judgment the Court concluded that transitioning from one sex to another was included in the protection offered against sex discrimination. More recently the Court has also recognised non-discrimination on the grounds of age to be a fundamental principle of Community law.[3]

This commitment to equal pay is now contained in Article 157 of the Treaty on the Functioning of the European Union (TFEU). It includes the principle of equal pay for male and female workers for equal work or for work of equal value. It also provides for the Community to adopt measures to ensure the application of the principle of equal opportunities and equal treatment of men and women in matters of employment and occupation, including the principle of equal pay for equal work or work of equal value.[4]

It was in 1975 that a Directive on equal pay was adopted[5] and an equal treatment Directive, concerning equality between men and women, was adopted the following year.[6] These and

---

1 Case C-149/77 *Defrenne v Sabena* (No 3).
2 Case C-13/94 *P v S and Cornwall County Council* [1996] IRLR 347 ECJ.
3 See Case C-144/04 *Mangold v Helm* [2006] IRLR 143.
4 Article 157(3).
5 Directive 1975/117/EC.
6 Directive 76/207/EC.

subsequent amending Directives have now been consolidated into Directive 2006/54/EC on the implementation of the principle of equal opportunities and equal treatment of men and women in matters of employment and occupation.

It was not until the year 2000 that Directives concerning other grounds of discrimination were adopted, most notably one concerning race discrimination.[7] This Directive was not limited to employment,[8] unlike a further Directive in the same year that concerned discrimination relating to age, disability, religion or belief and sexual orientation.[9] One of the motivating factors for these initiatives was, apparently, the fear of resurgent extremist nationalism in some EU Member States. This provided the political will for the Treaty to be amended in order to allow the adoption of these two Directives.[10]

Clearly these Directives have involved compromises between different member states during the adoption process, but it is a matter of some achievement that, as a result, all the Member States of the EU have national legislation making discrimination on the grounds of sex, racial or ethnic origin, age, disability, religion or belief and sexual orientation unlawful. There is also a further proposal to extend the measures contained in the 2000 Framework Directive to areas outside the field of employment,[11] although there is no certainty that this proposal will be adopted.

The general right for the EU to take action is now contained in Article 19 of the TFEU:

> Without prejudice to the other provisions of the Treaties and within the limits of the powers conferred by them upon the Union, the Council, acting unanimously . . . and after obtaining the consent of the European Parliament, may take appropriate action to combat discrimination based on sex, racial or ethnic origin, religion or belief, disability, age or sexual orientation.

Article 18 also prohibits discrimination on the basis of nationality.

2.2 The Equality Directives

There are five Directives that are considered here as relevant to understanding EU legislation on equality. They are Directive 2006/54/EC concerned with equality between men and women in employment, Directive 2010/41/EU on the application of the principle of equal treatment between men and women engaged in a self-employed capacity, Directive 2004/113/EC implementing the principle of equal treatment between men and women in the access to and supply of goods and services. There is also Directive 2000/43/EC, which implements the principle of equal treatment between persons irrespective of racial or ethnic origin, and Directive 2000/78/EC establishing a general framework for equal treatment in employment and occupation.

2.2.1 The Equal Opportunities and Equal Treatment Directive

Directive 2006/54/EC on the implementation of the principle of equal opportunities and equal treatment of men and women in matters of employment and occupation is a recast Directive replacing seven previous sex equality Directives, including the Equal Pay Directive 75/117, the Equal Treatment Directive 76/207 as amended by Directive 2002/73 and the Burden of Proof

---

7 Directive 2000/43/EC implementing the principle of equal treatment between persons irrespective of racial or ethnic origin.
8 In 2004 Directive 2004/113/EC implementing the principle of equal treatment between men and women in the access to and supply of goods and services expanded the scope of sex discrimination to the area of goods and services.
9 Directive 2000/78/EC establishing a general framework for equal treatment in employment and occupation.
10 See European Union Agency for Fundamental Rights (2010).
11 Proposal for a Council Directive on implementing the principle of equal treatment between persons irrespective of religion or belief, disability, age or sexual orientation COM(2008) 426.

Directive 97/80, with one consolidated Directive. Its purpose, contained in Article 1, is to ensure the implementation of the principle of equal opportunities and equal treatment of men and women in matters of employment and occupation. To achieve this it contains provisions in relation to: equal treatment with regard to access to employment, including promotion and vocational training; working conditions, including pay; and occupational social security schemes.

Article 2 is concerned with defining the meaning of discrimination and harassment amongst other terms; so direct discrimination is defined as 'where one person is treated less favourably on grounds of sex than another is, has been or would be treated in a comparable situation'. Indirect discrimination is defined as:

> where an apparently neutral provision, criterion or practice would put persons of one sex at a particular disadvantage compared with persons of the other sex, unless that provision, criterion or practice is objectively justified by a legitimate aim, and the means of achieving that aim are appropriate and necessary.

Thus it is possible to justify indirect discrimination (but not direct discrimination) by showing that the provision, criterion or practice is objectively justified by having a legitimate aim and that the means of achieving that aim are appropriate and necessary. It is interesting to note that the UK legislation implementing the Directive uses the word 'proportionate' rather than the words 'appropriate and necessary' (see Chapter 3). Seymour-Smith[12] was a case at the European Court of Justice that concerned the rule existing at the time that an employee with less than two years' continuous employment did not have the right to make a claim for unfair dismissal. One of the questions was whether the measure had a greater impact on women than men and could thus amount to indirect discrimination. The figures presented showed that 77.4 per cent of men qualified with two years' service compared to 68.9 per cent of women. The Court held that this did not seem to show a statistically significant difference. It was for the national court to make the judgment as to whether there was a significant impact of a particular measure. If this were so, then it would amount to indirect discrimination unless it could be objectively justified and shown that the measure was a proportionate means of achieving the legitimate aim. Just showing that the measure would advance a social policy aim (in this case encouraging recruitment) was not enough if it had the effect of discriminating on the grounds of sex.

In Directive 2006/54/EC there then follows a definition of harassment and, appropriately for a Directive concerned with equality between men and women, sexual harassment; so harassment is taken to mean a situation 'where unwanted conduct related to the sex of a person occurs with the purpose or effect of violating the dignity of a person, and of creating an intimidating, hostile, degrading, humiliating or offensive environment'. Sexual harassment is more specific and is where:

> any form of unwanted verbal, non-verbal or physical conduct of a sexual nature occurs, with the purpose or effect of violating the dignity of a person, in particular when creating an intimidating, hostile, degrading, humiliating or offensive environment.

Harassment and sexual harassment are specifically included in the definition of discrimination, as are instructions to discriminate on the grounds of sex and less favourable treatment of women in relation to pregnancy and maternity.[13]

---

12 Case 167/97 R v Secretary of State for Employment ex parte Seymour-Smith [1999] IRLR 253; see also Case C-127/92 Enderby v Frenchay Health Authority and Secretary of State for Health [1993] IRLR 51.
13 Article 2(2) Directive 2006/54/EC.

There is also provision for protection from victimisation.[14] Employees and their representatives are protected against dismissal or any other adverse action by the employer as 'a reaction to a complaint within the undertaking or to any legal proceedings aimed at enforcing compliance with the principle of equal treatment'. Thus protection is available if an employer takes action against an employee who makes a complaint about discrimination or takes or participates in related legal proceedings.

The Directive also has specific provisions on equal pay. There is a broad definition of what is meant by pay. Article 2(1)(e) provides that pay is 'the ordinary basic or minimum wage or salary and any other consideration, whether in cash or in kind, which the worker receives directly or indirectly, in respect of his/her employment from his/her employer'. Article 4(1) then establishes the principle of equal pay by stating that:

> For the same work or for work to which equal value is attributed, direct and indirect discrimina-
> tion on grounds of sex with regard to all aspects and conditions of remuneration shall be
> eliminated.

If a job classification system is used, then the criteria for evaluation must exclude any consideration of sex.

Article 14 provides for the prohibition of employment in relation to access to employment, vocational training, promotion and working conditions. Discrimination on the grounds of sex is prohibited in relation to:

(a) conditions for access to employment, to self-employment or to occupation, including selection criteria and recruitment conditions, whatever the branch of activity and at all levels of the professional hierarchy, including promotion;

(b) access to all types and to all levels of vocational guidance, vocational training, advanced vocational training and retraining, including practical work experience;

(c) employment and working conditions, including dismissals, as well as pay as provided for in Article 141 [157 TFEU] of the Treaty;

(d) membership of, and involvement in, an organisation of workers or employers, or any organisation whose members carry on a particular profession, including the benefits provided for by such organisations.

There is also specific provision for women returning from maternity leave. Article 15 provides that such women have the right to return to their previous job or one that was equivalent on terms no less favourable to them. They also have the right to benefit from any improvement in working conditions that have taken place during their absence.

The Directive also provides for an exception to the principle of non-discrimination in relation to occupational requirements and access to employment. It is possible to show that 'by reason of the nature of the particular occupational activities' having a requirement for someone of a particular sex is a 'genuine and determining occupational requirement', providing that the objective is legitimate and the requirement is proportionate. The opportunity for derogation from the Directive is to be strictly limited, however. In *Johnston*[15] the dispute concerned a female police officer in the Royal Ulster Constabulary (RUC) who was refused a renewal of her contract as a member of the RUC full-time reserve and was also (like other female officers) not allowed to be given training in the handling of firearms. The reason for this was the Chief Constable's view that the force employed

---

14 Article 24.
15 Case C-222/84 *Johnston v Chief Constable of the Royal Ulster Constabulary* [1986] IRLR 263.

sufficient women and that giving female officers the right to carry guns would endanger their lives.[16] The Court observed that any derogation 'from an individual right laid down in the directive, must be interpreted strictly'. In determining the scope of the derogation the principle of proportionality should be applied, in other words the derogation should be only that considered 'appropriate and necessary' to achieve the aim required, as well as needing to be reconciled with the principle of equal treatment.

2.2.2 Equal treatment for the self-employed

Directive 2010/41/EU replaced Directive 86/613/EEC and provides for the principle of equal treatment between men and women engaged in a self-employed capacity 'or contributing to the pursuit of such an activity'.[17] The Directive covers self-employed workers who are defined as 'all persons pursuing a gainful activity for their own account, under the conditions laid down by national law'.[18] It also protects the spouses of self-employed workers and, under the conditions laid down by national law, the life partners of the self-employed who habitually 'participate in the activities of the self-employed worker and perform the same tasks or ancillary tasks'.[19]

Article 4 provides that there should be no discrimination on the grounds of sex, for example in the 'establishment, equipment or extension of a business or the launching or extension of any form of self-employed activity'. Article 5 provides for the possibility of positive action 'with a view to ensuring full equality between men and women in working life, for instance aimed at promoting entrepreneurship initiatives among women'. Finally there is provision in Article 8 for female self-employed workers and female spouses and life partners to be granted maternity allowances for at least 14 weeks.

2.2.3 The Gender Equality Directive

Directive 2004/113/EC implementing the principle of equal treatment between men and women in the access to and supply of goods and services extended the scope of protection against sex discrimination outside the field of employment and vocational training. Article 1 provides that its purpose is:

> to lay down a framework for combating discrimination based on sex in access to and supply of goods and services, with a view to putting into effect in the Member States the principle of equal treatment between men and women.

The Directive provides a similar approach to prohibiting sex discrimination to that of Directive 2006/54/EC, discussed above, to those who provide goods and services 'offered outside the area of private and family life and the transactions carried out in this context'.

There are special issues of course, such as the prohibition of the use of sex in actuarial calculations.[20] It is not possible, for example, to say that women are better car drivers and thus reduce their insurance premiums when compared to men. The decision would be a sex-based one and not permissible. Prior to the end of 2012 the use of sex as a criterion in actuarial calculations was permitted in some Member States by Article 5(2) of the Directive, but this was stopped as a result

---

16 This has to be considered in the context of the violent conflict taking place in Northern Ireland at the time.
17 Article 1.
18 Article 2(a).
19 Article 2(b).
20 Article 5.

of a decision by the Court of Justice of the European Union (CJEU) in the case of *Achats*.[21] This case was a referral from the Belgian court and, according to the CJEU, was about whether Article 5(2) was valid in the light of the principle of equal treatment for men and women. In ruling that Article 5(2) was valid, the Court of Justice emphasised that the principle of equal treatment requires that comparable situations must not be treated differently and different situations must not be treated in the same way. There had been transitional provisions contained in the Directive, but Member States could not be allowed to perpetuate these temporary exceptions because of Article 5(2). Paradoxically, the effect of this judgment, according to press reports, was that car insurance premiums for women would actually increase.[22]

2.2.4 The Framework Directive for Equal Treatment in Employment and Occupation

Council Directive 2000/78/EC established a general framework for equal treatment in employment and occupation.[23] The purpose of the Directive is to put into effect in the Member States 'the principle of equal treatment as regards access to employment and occupation . . . of all persons irrespective of racial or ethnic origin, religion or belief, disability, age or sexual orientation'.[24] It is worth remembering that the provisions of the Directive are limited to employment and occupation and that there is a further Directive proposed to extend this protection to activities outside the field of employment.[25]

Article 3 is concerned with this scope and provides that the Directive applies to conditions for access to employment, which include selection criteria and recruitment conditions as well as promotion; access to vocational guidance, training and retraining, including practical work experience; employment and working conditions, including dismissals and pay as well as membership of workers' or employers' organisations. This is effectively applying similar provisions to discrimination on the grounds of age, disability, religion or belief and sexual orientation as are applied to sex discrimination in Directive 2006/54/EC.

There are, however, two areas of discrimination where there are extra provisions: these are age and disability. Article 5 states that:

> In order to guarantee compliance with the principle of equal treatment in relation to persons with disabilities, reasonable accommodation shall be provided. This means that employers shall take appropriate measures, where needed in a particular case, to enable a person with a disability to have access to, participate in, or advance in employment, or to undergo training, unless such measures would impose a disproportionate burden on the employer. This burden shall not be disproportionate when it is sufficiently remedied by measures existing within the framework of the disability policy of the Member State concerned.

Thus Article 5 provides for the duty of reasonable accommodation with respect to people with disabilities. This is more commonly referred to in the UK as the duty to make adjustments. Thus if a provision, criterion or practice is identified as causing disadvantage to those with disabilities, then

---

21 Case C-236/09 *Association Belge des Consommateurs Test-Achats*.
22 BBC news website, 1 March 2011, available at: http://www.bbc.co.uk/news/business-12606610 (last accessed 17 January 2013).
23 OJ L303/16 2.12.2000.
24 Article 1 of the Directive.
25 Proposal for a Council Directive on implementing the principle of equal treatment between persons irrespective of religion or belief, disability, age or sexual orientation COM2008 426.

the employer is obliged to make these reasonable adjustments.[26] There is also the scope for national legislation to exclude the armed forces from the provisions relating to age and disability.

Apart from this reference to age there are also other limitations placed on those wishing to claim age discrimination. Article 6 provides for a very broad range of exceptions with respect to the prohibition on age discrimination, including the possibility of objective justification for direct and indirect discrimination, the effect of which is to considerably weaken the impact of the Directive in this field. Article 6 states that:

> Member States may provide that differences of treatment on grounds of age shall not constitute discrimination, if, within the context of national law, they are objectively and reasonably justified by a legitimate aim, including legitimate employment policy, labour market and vocational training objectives, and if the means of achieving that aim are appropriate and necessary.
>
> Such differences of treatment may include, among others:
>
> (a) the setting of special conditions on access to employment and vocational training, employment and occupation, including dismissal and remuneration conditions, for young people, older workers and persons with caring responsibilities in order to promote their vocational integration or ensure their protection;
> (b) the fixing of minimum conditions of age, professional experience or seniority in service for access to employment or to certain advantages linked to employment;
> (c) the fixing of a maximum age for recruitment which is based on the training requirements of the post in question or the need for a reasonable period of employment before retirement.

A good example of how this allows exceptions in relation to age can be seen in the case of *Torsten Hörnfeldt*.[27] Mr Hörnfeldt began working for the postal service agency in 1989. Between 1989 and 2006 he worked one day per week; between 2006 and 2008 he worked 75 per cent of the time; between 11 October 2008 and 31 May 2009 he had a contract of indefinite duration but still only worked on a 75 per cent basis. He was retired when he reached the last day of the month in which he reached the age of 67 years. Differences of treatment on the grounds of age are permitted if they are objectively and reasonably justified by having a legitimate aim including legitimate employment, labour market and vocational training policy directives, and if the means of achieving that aim are appropriate and necessary. The Swedish law, however, made no precise mention of the aim pursued by the rule. This the CJEU said that this was not decisive. There may be other elements that enable the aim to be identified. The Swedish government argued that the compulsory retirement at age 67 rule:

(1) avoids the termination of employment contracts that may be humiliating for older workers;
(2) enables retirement pensions to be adjusted on the principle that income over the entire period of a career should be taken into account;
(3) reduces obstacles to those who wished to work after their 65th birthday;
(4) adapts to demographic changes and avoids a shortage of labour; and
(5) establishes a right, not an obligation, to work until the age of 67.

It also argued that fixing a compulsory retirement age makes it easier for young people to enter the labour market. The Court accepted all these as legitimate aims and that compulsory retirement was

---

26 Article 2(b)(ii).
27 Case C-141/11 *Hörnfeldt v Posten Meddelande AB* [2012] IRLR 785.

an appropriate and necessary means of achieving these aims. It means that compulsory retirement can be justified under the Directive, even though forcing someone to leave work because they have reached a certain age is a significant age discriminatory act (see Chapter 4).

The great majority of cases at the Court of Justice concerning this Directive have involved the age aspects of the prohibition on discrimination. An example of this is *Mangold v Rüdiger Helm*,[28] which concerned a rule that permitted older people to be employed on fixed-term contracts with no restrictions. Prior to the transposition of Directive 1999/70,[29] German law had placed a number of restrictions on fixed-term contracts of employment, requiring an objective reason justifying the fixed term or, alternatively, imposing limits on the number of contract renewals (a maximum of three) and on total duration (a maximum of two years).[30] These restrictions did not apply to contracts with people over the age of 52 years. Mr Mangold was employed on a fixed-term contract at the age of 56. Thus the question was that such a measure needed objective justification as required by Article 6 of Directive 2000/78/EC.

It was accepted that legislation that permitted employers to conclude, without restriction, fixed-term contracts with workers over the age of 52 did amount to a difference of treatment on the grounds of age. The Court readily accepted that 'purpose of that legislation is plainly to promote the vocational integration of unemployed older workers' and that 'the legitimacy of such a public-interest objective cannot reasonably be thrown in doubt'. There is no indication in the published Opinion of AG Tizzano or the Court's judgment that any evidence was considered with regard to this. The real difficulty for the Court was whether the means adopted were appropriate and necessary. The national court had doubted whether the measure was in compliance with the Directive and the Court of Justice agreed. The problem was that the rule applied to all workers who had reached the age of 52, whether or not they had been unemployed before the contract was concluded and whatever the duration of any period of unemployment. The Court concluded:

> This significant body of workers, determined solely on the basis of age, is thus in danger, during a substantial part of its members' working life, of being excluded from the benefit of stable employment which, however, as the Framework Agreement makes clear, constitutes a major element in the protection of workers.

Thus the measure went beyond what was appropriate and necessary in order to achieve the legitimate aim.

In *Maruko*[31] the ECJ considered its first case concerning the sexual orientation provisions of the Directive. This case concerned Mr Maruko, who had entered into a civil partnership in Germany. His life partner was a member of an occupational pension scheme and when he died, Mr Maruko claimed a widower's pension from the scheme. He was refused on the grounds that only spouses were provided for under the scheme's rules. He claimed discrimination on the grounds of sexual orientation and the issue was whether the provisions of such a scheme came within the scope of the Directive. The Court held that such a pension, which was related to employment and service, was part of the individual's pay and therefore was covered. In this case, therefore, Mr Maruko had been less favourably treated than surviving spouses and, as a result, had been discriminated against on the grounds of sexual orientation.

---

28 Case C-144/04 *Mangold*.
29 Directive 1999/70/EC concerning the framework agreement on fixed-term work concluded by ETUC, UNICE and CEEP.
30 The facts of this case are taken from the Opinion of AG Tizzano.
31 Case C-267/06 *Maruko v Versorgungsanstalt Der Deutschen Bühnen* [2008] IRLR 405.

2.2.5 The Race Directive

Council Directive 2000/43/EC implements the principle of equal treatment between persons irrespective of racial or ethnic origin.[32] This helped bring to an end the imbalance in the EU's anti-discrimination programme. In contrast to the EU's action on equal pay and sex discrimination, it has taken fewer initiatives to combat race discrimination. In their guidance to the Directive the European Commission accepts that racial discrimination is widespread in everyday life and that legal measures are of 'paramount importance for combating racism and intolerance'.[33]

The purpose of the Directive, contained in Article 1, is 'to lay down a framework for combating discrimination on the grounds of racial or ethnic origin, with a view to putting into effect in the Member States the principle of equal treatment'. Article 2 is concerned with the meaning of direct and indirect discrimination and follows the Framework Directive on Equal Treatment in Employment and Occupation Directive closely, including the addition of harassment. Its scope, of course, is wider than just employment, and includes other areas such as facilities, goods and services. Thus this wider scope of application is reserved for sex and race discrimination, although, as will be shown in the following chapters, the UK has gone further and extended the protection offered generally to include facilities, goods and services as well as employment protection.

In *Firma Feryn*[34] the complainant was the Belgian organisation that had been set up in accordance with Article 13 of the Directive to promote equality.[35] It had taken action against Firma Feryn NV, the respondent company. One of the directors of the company, which sold and installed up and over and sectional doors, had made a statement to the effect that, although the company was seeking to recruit, it could not employ 'immigrants' because its customers were reluctant to give them access to their private residences for the duration of the works. According to the report he said:

> I must comply with my customers' requirements. If you say 'I want that particular product or I want it like this and like that' and I say 'I am not doing it, I'll send those people', then they say 'I don't need that door'. Then I am putting myself out of business. We must meet the customers' requirements. This isn't my problem. I didn't create this problem in Belgium. I want the firm to do well and I want to achieve our turnover at the end of the year, and how do I do that? – I must do it the way the customer wants it done.

The question was whether this constituted direct discrimination as in Article 2(2)(a) of the Directive. Direct discrimination is concerned with treating someone les favourably than another on racial or ethnic grounds. Although this director had made these statements, there was no evidence that any individual had been treated less favourably or that anyone had been turned down for a job on the grounds of racial or ethnic origin. The CJEU relied upon Recital 8 of the Directive's preamble, which refers to the need to 'foster conditions for a socially inclusive labour market'. The Court said that this would be difficult to achieve if the Directive's scope was limited only to occasions when an individual made a complaint of direct discrimination. The Court held that such a statement concerning candidates of a particular ethnic or racial origin constituted direct discrimination under Article 2(2)(a) of Directive 2000/43. Such a public declaration was clearly likely to dissuade some candidates from applying for jobs with the employer, so there must be presumption of a discriminatory recruitment policy.

---

32 OJ L180/22 17.7.2000.
33 See also Council Regulation 1035/97 establishing a European Monitoring Centre on Racism and Xenophobia OJ L151 10.6.97.
34 Case C-54/07 *Centrum voor Gelijkeid voor Kansen en voor Racismebestrijding v Firma Feryn NV* [2008] IRLR 732.
35 Article 13(1) states that 'Member States shall designate a body or bodies for the promotion of equal treatment of all persons without discrimination on the grounds of racial or ethnic origin. These bodies may form part of agencies charged at national level with the defence of human rights or the safeguard of individuals' rights'; this is replicated in all the equality directives.

2.3 Facilities, goods and services

The EU has also been concerned with tackling discrimination outside of employment in those fields where this is not currently covered. Thus it has proposed a draft Equal Treatment Directive in relation to religion or belief, disability, age or sexual orientation.[36]

Article 1 of the proposed Directive sets out its purpose and states:

> This Directive lays down a framework for combating discrimination on the grounds of religion or belief, disability, age, or sexual orientation, with a view to putting into effect in the Member States the principle of equal treatment other than in the field of employment and occupation.

It follows the pattern of the Employment Directives by making direct and indirect discrimination and harassment unlawful and has the possibility of justification, namely that there should be a legitimate aim and the means of achieving that aim are appropriate and necessary, although as stated in Article 2(7):

> in the provision of financial services Member States may permit proportionate differences in treatment where, for the product in question, the use of age or disability is a key factor in the assessment of risk based on relevant and accurate actuarial or statistical data.

Article 3 provides the scope, which is that it applies the public and private sectors in relation to:

(a) social protection, including social security and health care;
(b) social advantages;
(c) education;
(d) access to and supply of goods and other services that are available to the public, including housing.

This proposal is not supported by all Member States so it may be some time before it is adopted.

2.4 Human rights

2.4.1 The European Convention on Human Rights

Article 6(2) of the TFEU provides that the EU will accede to the European Convention for the Protection of Human Rights and Fundamental Freedoms (the Convention). The Convention is an international treaty signed by members of the Council of Europe.[37] It was originally signed in 1950 and entered into force in 1953. The Convention consists of a number of Articles and Protocols but essentially (see website of the Council of Europe[38]) secures the right to life, the right to a fair hearing, the right to respect for private and family life, freedom of expression, freedom of thought, conscience and religion and the protection of property. In particular it prohibits torture and inhuman or degrading treatment or punishment, slavery and forced labour, the death penalty,

---

36 Proposal for a Council Directive on implementing the principle of equal treatment between persons irrespective of religion or belief, disability, age or sexual orientation, COM(2008) 426.
37 Available at: http://www.echr.coe.int/NR/rdonlyres/DF074FE4-96C2-4384-BFF6-404AAF5BC585/0/ENG_Court_in_brief.pdf (last accessed 17 January 2013).
38 http://hub.coe.int/.

arbitrary and unlawful detention, and discrimination in the enjoyment of the rights and freedoms set out in the Convention.

The European Court of Human Rights[39] is based in Strasbourg (as distinct from the European Court of Justice in Luxembourg) and was established in 1959. It rules on individual or state applications concerning potential violations of the rights set out in the Convention. Since it was established in 1959, the Court has delivered more than 15,000 judgments. Nearly half of the judgments concerned four Member States: Turkey (2,747), Italy (2,166), Russia (1,212) and Poland (945). Of the total number of judgments it has delivered since 1959, in over 83 per cent of cases the Court has found at least one violation of the Convention by the respondent State.[40] One of the striking differences between this Court and the European Court of Justice is the ability of private complainants and groups to make their complaints directly to the Court.

Article 14 of the Convention deals with discrimination and states that:

> The enjoyment of the rights and freedoms set forth in this Convention shall be secured without discrimination on any ground, such as sex, race, colour, language, religion, political or other opinion, national or social origin, association with a minority, property or other status.

There are two matters that we might note about this Article: first, the scope of its coverage and, second, the fact that it is not a free-standing right. The range of grounds of discrimination covered include a number that are not contained in UK legislation, such as 'political or other opinion' or 'social origin'. It is also an open-ended list. The words 'or other status' leave open the possibility of other grounds of discrimination that are not listed. The second issue refers to the opening phrase, namely 'the enjoyment of rights and freedoms set forth in this Convention shall be secured without discrimination'. This makes it clear that Article 14 is about securing the absence of discrimination in relation to the other Articles in the Convention. Thus it would be possible to bring a complaint under, say, Article 8 (the right to respect for private and family life) in conjunction with Article 14, but it would not be possible to bring a complaint under Article 14 on its own. This can be seen in the case of *Abdulaziz, Cabales and Balkandali v United Kingdom*.[41] The applicants were all lawfully resident in the United Kingdom, but Mr Abdulaziz, Mr Cabales and Mr Balkandali had been refused permission to join them or stay with them in the UK as their husbands. Amongst other matters they maintained that they had been victims of a practice of discrimination on the grounds of sex, race and also, in the case of Mrs Balkandali, birth, and that there had been violations of Article 3 (prohibition of torture) and of Article 8 (respect for private and family life), taken alone or in conjunction with Article 14. Paragraph 71 of the judgment stated that:

> According to the Court's established case-law, Article 14 (art. 14) complements the other substantive provisions of the Convention and the Protocols. It has no independent existence since it has effect solely in relation to 'the enjoyment of the rights and freedoms' safeguarded by those provisions. Although the application of Article 14 (art. 14) does not necessarily presuppose a breach of those provisions – and to this extent it is autonomous – there can be no room for its application unless the facts at issue fall within the ambit of one or more of the latter.

In the event the Court found that there had not been a violation of Article 8 on its own, but there had been a violation of Article 8 taken together with Article 14 and that the applicants had been

---

39 See http://www.echr.coe.int/ECHR/EN/Header/The+Court/Introduction/Information+documents/ (last accessed 17 January 2013).

40 Overview 1959–2011 (2012) European Court of Human Rights http://www.echr.coe.int/NR/rdonlyres/E58E405A-71CF-4863-91EE-779C34FD18B2/0/APERCU_19592011_EN.pdf (last accessed 17 January 2013).

41 Judgment of 28 May 1985; application nos. 9214/80; 9473/81; 9474/81 7 EHRR 471.

subject to discrimination on the grounds of sex. It is the combination of the Articles that is important. The claim for discrimination could not have been made unless it applied to one of 'the rights and freedoms' contained in one of the other Articles. Even though the claim failed concerning Article 8 alone, it was still possible to proceed with the combination claim and be successful.

In a more recent case, *Glor v Switzerland*,[42] the Court considered a claim combining Articles 8 and 14 in respect of disability. It is a slightly extraordinary case to the outsider. Mr Glor was deemed medically unfit to perform military service due to his diabetes. However, the authorities decided that Mr Glor's diabetes was not severe enough to relieve him from paying a non-negligible military service exemption tax on his annual earnings for several years to come. Mr Glor actually wanted to carry out his military service, but was stopped from doing so. He was not allowed to carry out the alternative civil service, as this was only available to conscientious objectors. Mr Glor argued that he had been subjected to discrimination on the basis of his disability because he had been prohibited from carrying out his military service, and was still obliged to pay the exemption tax as his disability was judged not to be severe enough for him not to pay it. In its judgment, the Court held that the Swiss government had violated Mr Glor's rights under Article 14 in conjunction with Article 8. The Court noted that an individual's physical integrity relates to the exercise of a person's right to private and family life as set out in Article 8. In the present case, a tax levied by the State that finds its origin in a person's inability to serve in the army due to disability, something that is beyond the applicant's ability to control, falls within the scope of Article 8 of the Convention even if the consequences of the measures are primarily monetary.

2.4.2 Charter of Fundamental Rights of the EU

The Charter of Fundamental Rights of the European Union was proclaimed in December 2000. Article 6(1) of the TFEU states that:

> The Union recognises the rights, freedoms and principles set out in the Charter of Fundamental Rights . . . which will have the same legal value as the Treaties.

Protocol 30, Article 1(1) of the TFEU provides that:

> The Charter does not extend the ability of the Court of Justice of the European Union or any court or tribunal of Poland or of the United Kingdom to find that the laws, regulations or admin-istrative provisions, practices or action of Poland or the United Kingdom are inconsistent with the fundamental rights, freedoms and principles that it reaffirms.

This has been referred to as the United Kingdom opt-out from the provisions of the Charter, although this does not seem to be what Protocol 30 says. It certainly limits the effectiveness of the Charter by limiting its impact in the UK and Poland. The problem for these governments (and the Czech Republic) at the time the Charter was adopted in 2000 was that it does not only contain what might be regarded as traditional rights and freedoms such as equal treatment for men and women, but also social and political rights that might limit the policies of national governments, such as the right to take industrial action, contained in Article 28.

---

42 Information taken from the website of the Mental Disability Advocacy Centre http://www.mdac.info/en/news/three-disability-%E2%80%98firsts%E2%80%99-european-court-human-rights-case (last accessed 17 January 2013). The case report on the Court of Human Rights website is in French only.

The rights given in the Charter are divided into six sections: dignity, freedom, equality, solidarity, citizen's rights and justice.[43] The Preamble states the rationale for the Charter:

> Conscious of its spiritual and moral heritage, the Union is founded on the indivisible, universal values of human dignity, freedom, equality and solidarity; it is based on the principles of democracy and the rule of law. It places the individual at the heart of its activities, by establishing the citizenship of the Union and by creating an area of freedom, security and justice.

Title III is concerned with equality and Article 21 provides that there should be no discrimination based on any ground 'such as' sex, race, colour, ethnic or social origin, genetic features, language, religion or belief, political or other opinion, membership of a national minority, property, birth, disability, age, sexual orientation and nationality. The phrase 'such as' suggests that this is not a closed list but an open-ended one, so further grounds could be considered. Even so the list is substantial and much greater than that contained in UK legislation. Other Articles in this part include Article 22, which is about respect for cultural, religious and linguistic diversity, Article 23 concerning equality between men and women, Article 25 on the rights of the elderly and Article 26 concerning the integration of persons with disabilities.

2.5 Summary

The question here is about the role of international organisations and treaties. Is it fair that some countries can opt out of agreements as the UK did with the Charter of Fundamental Rights?

This chapter has shown that eventually the EU has been able to legislate on protection in relation to discrimination on the grounds of sex, race, disability, age, region or belief and sexual orientation. The legislation concerns a closed list of protected grounds unlike the more open-ended European Convention. What are the advantages and disadvantages of these different approaches?

It is interesting to speculate as to whether the UK would have any age discrimination legislation were it not for the Framework Directive. It is also clear that other Member States would not have national measures concerning discrimination on such grounds as disability, religion or belief and sexual orientation were it not for the necessity of transposing European Directives on the subject.

---

43 The Charter has its own web pages at http://www.europarl.europa.eu/charter/default_en.htm (last accessed 17 January 2013); a good explanation of each of the Articles can also be found at http://www.europarl.europa.eu/charter/pdf/04473_en.pdf (last accessed 17 January 2013).

Chapter 3

The Equality Act 2010

Chapter Contents

3.1 Introduction

The Equality Act 2010 replaced a number of pieces of other legislation, such as the Sex Discrimination Act (SDA) 1975, the Race Relations Act (RRA) 1976 and the Disability Discrimination Act 1995. It also replaced a number of Regulations that made discrimination in relation to employment on the grounds of age, religion or belief and sexual orientation unlawful. It is, therefore, the most important piece of UK legislation concerned with tackling discrimination. The Equality and Human Rights Commission (EHRC) has the power to issue Codes of Practice whose purpose is the elimination of discrimination in the field of employment or for the promotion of equality.[1] Section 15(4) of the Equality Act 2006 provides that in relation to such statutory Codes of Practice:

> A failure to comply with a provision of a code shall not of itself make a person liable to criminal or civil proceedings; but a code—
>
> (a)   shall be admissible in evidence in criminal or civil proceedings, and
> (b)   shall be taken into account by a court or tribunal in any case in which it appears to the court or tribunal to be relevant.

There are two important Codes that have been issued by the Commission, one on employment (EHRC 2011a) and one on equal pay (EHRC 2011b).

3.2 The protected characteristics

Section 4 of the Equality Act 2010 lists the nine protected characteristics with which the Act is concerned. These are further defined in sections 5–12. The protected characteristics are:

Age – a person belonging to a particular age group is protected. Age group means persons of the same age or persons of a range of ages, so an age group could be the 'over fifties' or just 'fifty-year-olds' or 'twenty-one-year-olds'.

Disability – this defines who is to be regarded as having the protected characteristic of disability. The provisions are similar to those that were contained in the Disability Discrimination Act 1995, so section 6(1) provides that a person has a disability if he or she has a physical or mental impairment that has a substantial and long-term adverse effect on his or her ability to carry out normal day-to-day activities.

Gender reassignment – a person has this protected characteristic if they are proposing to undergo, are undergoing or have undergone a process (or part of a process) for the purpose of reassigning the person's sex by changing physiological or other attributes of sex. A man transitioning to being a woman and a woman transitioning to being a man both share the characteristic of gender reassignment. Section 7(2) provides that all transsexual people are included. These provisions are similar to those in the Sex Discrimination Act 1975, except that there is no longer a need for the person to be under medical supervision in order to come within the definition.

Marriage and civil partnership – this applies to those that are married or in a civil partnership, so just living together is not enough. Examples of those who would not have this characteristic are a person who is only engaged to be married, or a person who has divorced his or her partner or had the civil partnership dissolved.

---

1   Section 14 Equality Act 2006.

Pregnancy and maternity – this protects people from discrimination on the grounds of pregnancy or any illness arising from that pregnancy. It also applies to taking or exercising rights under maternity leave provisions contained in section 18.

Race – this includes colour, nationality and ethnic or national origin. Those who have any of these characteristics can be described as a 'racial group' and the fact that a racial group consists of two or more racial groups does not prevent it from constituting a racial group. Section 9(5)(5) also allows the Minister to amend the Act so as to add 'caste' to the definition of race. Caste broadly means a hereditary community associated with a traditional occupation and ranked according to a perceived scale of ritual purity. It is generally, but not exclusively, associated with South Asia and particularly India and its diaspora.

Religion or belief – religion means any religion or lack of religion; belief means any philosophical belief or lack of such belief. The Guidance suggests that a religion must have a clear structure and belief system and that denominations within a religion can be considered to be a religion or belief, such as Protestants and Catholics within Christianity. The Guidance states that atheism or humanism would be included as beliefs, but not 'adherence to a particular football team'.

Sex – this section (11) is a new provision and provides that references in the Act to the protected characteristic of sex means being a man or a woman; men share this characteristic with other men and women with other women.

Sexual orientation – this is similar to the provisions of the Employment Equality (Sexual Orientation) Regulations 2003, so sexual orientation means a sexual orientation towards people of the same sex (applying to gay men and lesbians), the opposite sex, (applying to heterosexuals) or either sex (bisexuals). Thus a man and a woman attracted to people of the opposite sex share a sexual orientation, as do men only attracted to men and women who are only attracted to women; both of these latter groups share a sexual orientation.

The Equality Act 2010 also provides for the possibility of claims for dual discrimination in section 14 (see Chapter 1), but the coalition government elected in 2010 chose not to implement this measure, so multiple discrimination claims are difficult.

3.3 Prohibited conduct

The Act defines the conduct that is prohibited in relation to the protected characteristics.

3.3.1 Direct discrimination

Section 13(1) describes direct discrimination in the following way:

> a person (A) discriminates against another (B) if, because of a protected characteristic, A treats
> B less favourably than A treats, or would treat, others.

Previous legislation had used the term 'on the grounds of'. This is replaced by the term 'because of'. The Guidance to the legislation explained that this means the same but it is designed to make it more accessible.

Thus, direct discrimination occurs where, because of one of the protected characteristics, a person is treated less favourably than someone who does not share that characteristic would be treated. This would cover situations where there has been a generalised assumption that people in a particular group possess or lack certain characteristics. In *James v Eastleigh Borough Council*[2] the court asked the question whether the complainant would have received the same treatment from the defendant but for his or her sex. In this case a local authority gave free use of its swimming pools to persons of pensionable age. At the time the state retirement age for men was 65 years and for women it was 60 years. The male of 61 years, who had not reached pensionable age, was held to have suffered discrimination in comparison with a woman who reached it at the age of 60 years. Thus the 'but for' test can be applied where the treatment given derives from the application of gender-based criteria and where the treatment given results from the selection of the complainant because of his or her sex.

There does not need to be an intention to discriminate. In *R v Birmingham City Council, ex parte Equal Opportunities Commission*[3] the local authority offered more places in selective secondary education to boys than to girls. This was held to be treating those girls less favourably on the grounds of their sex and the fact that the local authority had not intended to discriminate was not relevant.

The definition in section 13(1) requires less favourable treatment in comparison to another or in comparison to the way that A 'would treat others'. Thus, in the absence of an actual comparator it is possible to use a hypothetical one. An exact comparator is not needed, of course, as it might be impossible to prove less favourable treatment, especially in isolated cases, if this were the case.[4]

The Equality Act 2010 elaborates in respect of direct discrimination and specific protected characteristics.

3.3.1.1 Age

As in the previous statute, section 13(2) provides that direct discrimination in relation to age can be justified if shown to be a proportionate means of achieving a legitimate aim. Age is the only protected characteristic for which it is possible to justify direct discrimination.

It is interesting to speculate why it is possible to justify direct discrimination with regard to age. The probable answer is that there are many circumstances where society accepts that discrimination on the grounds of age might be necessary and acceptable, for example in placing restrictions on the ability of school children under the age of 16 years to work; or in relation to special protection given to young people at work in terms of health and safety by controlling their hours of work and rest breaks. Without special provisions these measures might turn out to amount to age discrimination by effectively treating older people less favourably than the young workers concerned. It might, however, have been better to specify the exceptions rather than allowing the general possibility of justifying direct age discrimination (see Chapter 4).

3.3.1.2 Disability

Section 13(3) makes it clear that treating a person with a disability more favourably does not amount to discrimination against a person who does not have a disability.

The reason for this seems obvious, but it is important to ensure that more favourable treatment given to people with a disability, perhaps to enable an individual to compete on equal terms with a person without a disability, do not amount to treating someone else less favourably in comparison with the person with a disability. The Equality Act 2010 does provide for the duty to make reasonable adjustments for disabled people and also allows for claims to be brought on the ground of 'unfavourable' treatment, rather than 'less favourable', so there are some strong positive messages about stopping discrimination because of this protected characteristic (Chapter 5).

---

2 [1990] IRLR 288.
3 [1989] IRLR 173.
4 See *Balamoody v UK Central Council for Nursing* [2002] IRLR 288 CA.

3.3.1.3 Race

Less favourable treatment in relation to race includes segregation of a person from others[5] (see Chapter 7). Thus, when the protected characteristic is race, deliberately segregating a worker or group of workers from others of a different race automatically amounts to less favourable treatment. There is no need to identify a comparator, because racial segregation is always discriminatory.[6] The Code of Practice on Employment (EHRC 2011a) provides the following example:

> A British marketing company that employs predominantly British staff recruits Polish nationals and seats them in a separate room nicknamed 'Little Poland'. The company argues that they have an unofficial policy of seating the Polish staff separately from British staff so that they can speak amongst themselves in their native language without disturbing the staff who speak English. This is segregation, as the company has a deliberate policy of separating staff because of race.

3.3.1.4 Sex

In the case of sex discrimination, no account is to be taken of any special treatment given to a woman in connection with pregnancy or childbirth (section 13(6)).

Pregnancy, childbirth and maternity constitute a specially protected period (see Chapter 6). Clearly measures intended to protect women during this period will in practice amount to more favourable treatment and this section stops this special treatment being the grounds for complaint by others.

3.3.1.5 Examples of direct discrimination

The Guidance gives some examples of direct discrimination in practice, including:

> If an employer recruits a man rather than a woman because she assumes that women do not have the strength to do the job, this would amount to direct sex discrimination.

> If an employer rejects a job application form from a white man whom he wrongly thinks is black, because the applicant had an African-sounding name, this would constitute direct race discrimination based upon the employer's mistaken perception.

The Guidance also states that the definition of direct discrimination is broad enough to include those treated less favourably because of their association with someone who has the characteristic or because the victim is thought to have it. This is shown to be the case in *Coleman v Attridge Law*,[7] which interpreted European Community law as extending protection from discrimination to those associated with an individual, rather than to just the individual alone. In this case a mother of a child with a disability claimed successfully that she was protected by the Disability Discrimination Act 1995 even though she was not herself disabled. She had been obliged to take a lot of time off work to look after her child.

3.3.2 Indirect discrimination

Indirect discrimination is defined in section 19(1) as:

> A person (A) discriminates against another (B) if (A) applies to (B) a provision, criterion or practice which is discriminatory in relation to a relevant characteristic of (B)'s.

---

5 Section 13(5) Equality Act 2010.
6 Para 3.8 Code of Practice on Employment.
7 *Coleman v Attridge Law* [2008] IRLR 722.

Thus it occurs, according to the Guidance, when a policy that applies in the same way for every-body has an effect that particularly disadvantages people with a protected characteristic. Where a particular group is disadvantaged in this way, a person in that group is indirectly discriminated against if he or she is put at a disadvantage, unless A can show that it is a proportionate means of achieving a legitimate aim. Where a prima facie case of indirect discrimination has been estab-lished, the employer will have to satisfy the tribunal that the discriminatory requirement or condi-tion (provision, criterion or practice) was justifiable.

Indirect discrimination applies to all the protected characteristics except for pregnancy and maternity.

Section 19(2) provides that a provision, criterion or practice is discriminatory if, in relation to a protected characteristic of B's:

- first, A applies, or would apply, it to persons with whom B does not share the characteristic;
- second, that it puts, or would put, persons with whom B shares a characteristic at a particular disadvantage when compared with persons with whom B does not share that characteristic;
- third it puts, or would put, B at that disadvantage;
- finally, it cannot be justified by A showing it to be a proportionate means of achieving a legiti-mate aim.

These are all logical steps in the process of showing that a provision, criterion or practice is discriminatory. First, it is something that applies to others besides those who have the protected characteristic that it is claimed suffers discrimination. Then there is the requirement that people of a particular protected characteristic are put at a disadvantage compared to others, then that disadvantage is suffered by the claimant, and finally there is the possibility of objective justification.

Here is an example of indirect discrimination taken from the Guidance to the Equality Bill 2010, which illustrates the provision:

> A woman is forced to leave her job because her employer operates a practice that staff must work in a shift pattern that she is unable to comply with because she needs to look after her children at particular times of the day, and no allowances are made because of those needs. This would put women (who are shown to be more likely to be responsible for childcare) at a disadvantage, and the employer will have indirectly discriminated against the woman unless the practice can be justified.

In this case the provision, criterion or practice is the requirement that all staff work a shift pattern. This is a seemingly neutral requirement, but it has the effect of putting women at a disadvantage because they are more likely than men to have child care responsibilities that make shift work impossible.[8]

This is provided that the application of the 'provision, criterion or practice' cannot be shown to be justifiable irrespective of the sex of the person to whom it is applied. Each situation needs to be looked at on its own merits. Just because a policy might be gender-neutral in some situations, it does not follow that it will be so in all situations. *Whiffen v Milham Ford Girls' School*,[9] for example, concerned a school that followed its local educational authority's model redundancy policy. This

---

8 As in *London Underground v Edwards* [1998] IRLR 364.
9 [2001] IRLR 468 CA.

required that the non-renewal of temporary fixed-term contracts should be the first step to be taken. In this particular case, however, the result was indirectly to discriminate against female employees because 100 per cent of male employees could satisfy the condition that an employee needed to be on a permanent contract in order for their employment not to be terminated early, but only 77 per cent of female employees could satisfy this condition.

It is not enough to show that the employer's requirements have resulted in a detriment. There is a need for a detriment to be shown. In *Shamoon*,[10] for example, a female chief inspector was stopped from doing staff appraisals after some complaints about the manner in which she carried them out. When she complained of sex discrimination, the House of Lords ruled that a detriment occurs if a reasonable worker would or might take the view that they had been disadvantaged in the circumstances in which they had to work. However, it is not necessary to demonstrate some physical or economic consequence.

Seymour-Smith[11] was a case referred to the European Court of Justice on the legal test for establishing whether a measure adopted by a Member State has such a degree of disparate effect as between men and women as to amount to indirect discrimination for the purposes of Article 119 (now Article 157 TFEU) of the EC Treaty, unless shown to be based on objectively justified factors other than sex. The Court of Justice responded[12] by stating that, when attempting to establish whether there was indirect discrimination, the first question to ask was whether the measure under discussion had a more unfavourable impact on women than on men. After this it was a question of statistics by comparing the relative proportions of men and women who were affected. The Court decided that the statistics did not indicate a significant difference, although it was accepted that such measures should be reviewed from time to time.[13] At the time there was a requirement that an employee have two years continuous employment before unfair dismissal could be claimed. The case was about whether this amounted to indirect sex discrimination. The government argued, in justification, that it would encourage recruitment as some employers were reluctant to employ new staff without this requirement.

3.3.3 Harassment

Section 26(1) of the Equality Act 2010 provides that:

A person (A) harasses another if –

(a)   A engages in unwanted conduct related to a relevant protected characteristic, and

(b)   The conduct has the purpose or effect of –

(i) violating B's dignity, or

(ii) creating an intimidating, hostile, degrading, humiliating or offensive environment for B.

Examples given in the Guidance include:

A white worker who sees a black colleague being subjected to racially abusive language could have a case of harassment if the language also causes an offensive environment for her.

---

10 *Shamoon v Chief Constable of the RUC* [2003] IRLR 285.
11 *R v Secretary of State for Employment, ex parte Seymour-Smith and Perez (No 2)* [2000] IRLR 263.
12 Case C-167/97 [1999] IRLR 253 at p. 278.
13 The need to assess provisions periodically in the light of social developments was made by the European Court of Justice (ECJ) in *Commission v United Kingdom* [1984] IRLR 29.

> An employer who displayed any material of a sexual nature, such as a topless calendar, may be harassing her employees where this makes the workplace an offensive place to work for any employee, female or male.

There are three types of harassment provided for in the Equality Act 2010, the first of which applies to all protected characteristics except for pregnancy and maternity, and marriage and civil partnership:

- A engages in unwanted conduct related to a relevant protected characteristic that has the purpose or effect of violating B's dignity, or creating an intimidating, hostile, degrading, humiliating or offensive environment for B;[14]
- A engages in any form of unwanted verbal, non-verbal or physical conduct of a sexual nature that has that effect (section 26(2));
- Because of B's rejection of or submission to conduct (whether A's or not) related to sex or gender reassignment, A treats B less favourably than B would have been treated if B had not rejected or submitted to the conduct (section 26(3)).

So section 26(2) states that unwanted conduct of a sexual nature that has the outcome violating B's dignity, or creating an intimidating, hostile, degrading, humiliating or offensive environment for B, amounts to harassment. If B rejects, or refuses to submit to, such conduct (relating to sex or gender reassignment) then any subsequent less favourable treatment resulting from the rejection or refusal to submit may also amount to harassment.[15] The essential characteristic of sexual harassment is that it is words or conduct that are unwelcome to the recipient and it is for the recipient to decide for themselves what is acceptable to them and what they regard as offensive.[16] A characteristic of sexual harassment is that it undermines the victim's dignity at work and creates an 'offensive' or 'hostile' environment for the victim.

The complainant's perception is therefore of the utmost importance. That perception should not be dismissed just because the tribunal does not think that the actions of the respondent amounted to sexual harassment. There still needs to be evidence of harassment and the difficulty experienced by both parties is illustrated in British Telecommunications plc v Williams.[17] The complaint in this case arose out of a one-to-one counselling interview between a male manager and a female clerical officer. They were in close proximity; for example there was only one copy of the appraisal, which they had to share. It was alleged that the manager was sexually aroused and that she was effectively trapped in the interview room with him and that this amounted to sexual harassment. The employment tribunal accepted that the manager was not sexually aroused, but that the atmosphere at the interview was sexually intimidating. The Employment Appeal Tribunal (EAT) allowed the appeal. Proof of sexual harassment would cause a detriment, but having rejected the evidence on which the claim was made, that is that the manager was sexually aroused, it could not be said that there was sexual harassment. The alternative was that all female employees should have a chaperone whenever they had an interview with a male manager.

The Code of Practice on Employment Para 7.18 (EHRC 2011a) states that in deciding whether the conduct has the effect of violating B's dignity, or creating an intimidating, hostile, degrading, humiliating or offensive environment, the following factors need to be taken into account:

---

14 In relation to the protected characteristics of age, disability, gender reassignment, race, religion or belief, sex or sexual orientation.
15 Section 26(3) Equality Act 2010.
16 Section 26(4) Equality Act 2010.
17 [1997] IRLR 668.

(a)   The perception of the worker, that is, did they regard it as violating their dignity or creating an intimidating (etc.) environment for them. This part of the test is a subjective question and depends on how the worker regards the treatment.

(b)   The other circumstances of the case. Circumstances that may be relevant and therefore need to be taken into account can include the personal circumstances of the worker experiencing the conduct, for example, the worker's health, including mental health; mental capacity; cultural norms; or previous experience of harassment; and also the environment in which the conduct takes place.

(c)   The other circumstances of the case. Circumstances that may be relevant and therefore need to be taken into account can include the personal circumstances of the worker experiencing the conduct, for example, the worker's health, including mental health; mental capacity; cultural norms; or previous experience of harassment; and also the environment in which the conduct takes place.

In *Richmond Pharmacology Ltd v Dhaliwal*,[18] a racial harassment case, the EAT put the process more simplistically. The three elements of liability, according to the EAT, were:

1.   Whether the employer was engaged in unwanted conduct.
2.   Whether the conduct had (a) the purpose, or (b) the effect of either violating the claimant's dignity or creating an adverse environment for her.
3.   Whether the conduct was on the grounds of the claimant's race.

3.4 Harassment by third parties

Section 40(2) Equality Act 2010 provides that an employer can be liable for harassment of job applicants or employees by a third party such as a client or a customer. This is provided that the employer failed 'to take such steps as would have been reasonably practicable to prevent the third party from doing so'.[19] The duty to take such steps only arises after the applicant or employee has been harassed by a third party on at least two previous occasions.

The Code of Practice on Employment Para 10.20 (EHRC 2011a) provides this example:

A Ghanaian shop assistant is upset because a customer has come into the shop on Monday and Tuesday and on each occasion has made racist comments to him. On each occasion the shop assistant complained to his manager about the remarks. If his manager does nothing to stop it happening again, the employer would be liable for any further racial harassment perpetrated against that shop assistant by any customer.

3.4.1 Victimisation

Section 27(1) of the Equality Act 2010 provides that:

A person (A) victimises another person (B) if A subjects B to a detriment because

(a)   B does a protected act or
(b)   A believes that B has done, or may do, a protected act.

---

18 [2009] IRLR 336.
19 Section 40(2)(b) Equality Act 2010.

Protected act means bringing proceedings under this Act; giving evidence or information in connection with any proceedings under the Act; doing any other thing for the purpose of or in connection with this Act; making an allegation that A or another person has contravened the Act (section 27(2)). Giving false information or evidence is not protected if the information or evidence is given, or the allegation is made, in bad faith (section 27(3)).

The important change here, compared to previous legislation, is that, according to the Guidance, victimisation is no longer treated as a form of discrimination. There is therefore no need for a comparator.

Two examples given in the Guidance include:

A woman makes a complaint of sex discrimination against her employer. As a result, she is denied promotion. The denial of promotion would amount to victimisation.

An employer threatens to dismiss a staff member because he thinks she intends to support a colleague's sexual harassment claim. This threat could amount to victimisation.

In *St Helens Metropolitan Borough Council v Derbyshire*[20] the court held that whether victimisation had taken place was to be seen primarily from the perspective of the alleged victim, whether or not they have suffered detriment, not from the perspective of the alleged discriminator. In this case a number of employees brought an equal pay claim. Before the equal pay claims were due to be heard, the employers sent letters to the employees stating that they were concerned about the impact of the claim on staff.

3.5 Burden of proof

A real problem for those who feel that they have been a victim of a discriminatory act is actually being able to prove that it took place. In order to help with this process the relevant EU Directives (see Chapter 2) include provisions for a 'reversal' of the burden of proof. The complainant need only demonstrate that there is a prima facie case showing that discrimination has taken place. It is then for the respondent to show that this was not so.

Council Directive 97/80/EC on the burden of proof in cases of discrimination based on sex[21] was adopted by the Member States other than the United Kingdom in 1997. It was adopted by the United Kingdom, via an extension Directive,[22] in 1998. It is now included in Directive 2006/54 and has been extended to cover other protected characteristics. So, for example, Article 10(1) of the Equal Treatment in Employment and Occupation Directive states:

Member States shall take such measures as are necessary, in accordance with their national judicial systems, to ensure that, when persons who consider themselves wronged because the principle of equal treatment has not been applied to them establish, before a court or other competent authority, facts from which it may be presumed that there has been direct or indirect discrimination, it shall be for the respondent to prove that there has been no breach of the principle of equal treatment.

Section 136 of the Equality Act 2010 provides for this reversal of the normal requirements to prove a complaint. Section 136(2) states that:

---

20 [2007] IRLR 540.
21 OJ L14/6 20.1.98 (Burden of Proof Directive).
22 Council Directive 98/52/EC OJ L205/66 22.7.98.

If there are facts from which the court could decide, in the absence of any other explanation, that a person (A) contravened the provision concerned, the court must hold that the contravention occurred.

According to the Court of Appeal, very little direct discrimination is overt or deliberate. Often the employment tribunal will need to draw inferences as to the conduct of individuals in a particular case. In *King v The Great Britain–China Centre*[23] an applicant who was Chinese, but educated in Britain, failed to be short-listed for a post of deputy director of the Centre, even though her qualifications on paper seemed to meet the selection criteria. In such a situation the tribunal was entitled to look to the employer for an explanation. In this case none of the five ethnic Chinese candidates was selected for interview and the Centre had never employed a person with such an ethnic background. The Court of Appeal supported the approach of the employment tribunal in inferring that there was discrimination on racial grounds. In *King*, Neill LJ set down some principles and guidance that could be obtained from the authorities.[24] These were that:

1. It is for the applicant who complains of racial discrimination to make out his case.
2. It is unusual to find direct evidence of racial discrimination.
3. The outcome of a case will therefore usually rely upon what inferences it is possible to draw from the primary facts as found by the tribunal.
4. There will be some cases where it is possible to draw the inference of discrimination and in such cases the tribunal is entitled to look to the employer for an explanation.
5. It is unnecessary to introduce shifting evidential burdens of proof. Having adopted this approach then it is open to the tribunal to reach a conclusion based on the balance of probabilities.

In *Hewage v Grampian Health Board*[25] the Supreme Court considered an appeal against a finding of both sex and race discrimination against the employer. The court relied on the judgment in *Igen Ltd v Wong*,[26] which was an important case where the Court of Appeal considered a number of questions in relation to the interpretation of the statutes concerning the shifting of the burden of proof. The court held that the provisions required an employment tribunal to go through a two-stage process. The first stage is for the applicant to prove facts from which the tribunal could conclude, in the absence of an adequate explanation, that the respondent has committed an act of discrimination against the applicant. The second stage, which only comes into effect if the complainant has proved these facts, requires the respondent to prove that he did not commit the unlawful act. This case actually contains a 13-point guidance to the decision-making process in relation to the burden of proof. It includes:

1. The claimant must prove on the balance of probabilities facts so that, in the absence of an adequate explanation, the tribunal could conclude that the act of discrimination had taken place against the applicant.
2. It is unusual to find evidence of direct discrimination.
3. It could mean that at this stage the tribunal does not have to have reached a final conclusion.
4. The respondent must prove on the balance of probabilities that the treatment was not on a discriminatory ground.

---

23 [1991] IRLR 513 CA.
24 See now s 63A SDA 1975 and s 54A RRA 1976.
25 *Hewage v Grampian Health Board* [2012] IRLR 870.
26 [2005] IRLR 258.

The importance of shifting the burden of proof to the respondent once a prima facie case of discrimination has been established is of great importance. In *Madarassy v Nomura International plc*[27] the Court of Appeal stated:

> I do not underestimate the significance of the burden of proof in discrimination cases. There is probably no other area of civil law in which the burden of proof plays a larger part than in discrimination cases.

The Court in *Hewage* also relied on Mummery LJ's guidance in *Madarassy* that, from a practical point of view, even though a two-stage procedure was required by statute, the tribunal does not hear the evidence and the argument in two stages. In *Brown v LB of Croydon*[28] the court held that it was not obligatory, but good practice to do so. In some circumstances it was possible to go straight to the second stage. In this case the emphasis had been on the reasons for the treatment, so it was natural to do so.

There is a need to establish a causal relationship between the detriment and the racial or sexual discrimination. Mummery J discussed causation in *O'Neill*:[29] the tribunal's approach should be 'simple, pragmatic and commonsensical', although this approach needs to be qualified by the fact that the event complained of need not be the only or the main cause of the result complained of.

3.6 Equality of terms

Part 5, Chapter 3 of the Equality Act 2010 contains provisions aimed at achieving equality between men and women in pay and other terms of employment. There is also a Code of Practice on Equal Pay (EHRC 2011b). The Code states that the purpose of the equal pay provisions in the Equality Act 2010 are to ensure that pay and other employment conditions are determined without sex discrimination or bias. Historically, women 'have often been paid less than men for doing the same or equivalent work and this inequality has persisted in some areas'.

There are two further measures aimed at helping to reduce the gap in terms of employment between men and women. These are to persuade employers to publish information and protect the exchange of information between employees. Section 78 enables the Minister to make regulations requiring employers with at least 250 employees to publish information about the differences in pay between their male and female employees. In order to encourage employers to do this on a voluntary basis, the exercise of the power to make regulations will not take place before April 2013.

Any term of a person's work that tries to prevent the person from disclosing or seeking to disclose information about his or her work is unenforceable in relation to making pay disclosures (section 77). Thus the protected disclosure is not restricted to discussions with colleagues but could include other discussions, for example with a trade union representative. Any action that the employer takes against the employee as a result of this protection will be treated as victimisation (see section 27 above).

---

27 *Madarassy v Nomura International plc* [2007] IRLR 246.
28 [2007] IRLR 259.
29 *O'Neill v Governors of St Thomas More Roman Catholic Voluntarily Aided Upper School* [1996] IRLR 372.

3.7 Remedies

Complaints to an employment tribunal must be brought within three months beginning with the date on which the act complained of took place, unless the employment tribunal thinks that some other period is 'just and equitable' (section 123(1) Equality Act 2010). The complainant is able to obtain information by using the prescribed questionnaire and the questions and answers are admissible as evidence at the court or tribunal. The court or tribunal may draw inferences from a failure to answer within eight weeks or from evasive or equivocal answers.

If the employment tribunal finds that there has been a contravention of a provision, then it may:

(a)   make a declaration as to the rights of the complainant and the respondent in relation to the complainant;

(b)   order the respondent to pay compensation to the complainant;

(c)   make an appropriate recommendation.

There is no statutory upper limit for compensation in discrimination claims or those concerned with a breach of the equality clause.

Thus the tribunal or court may make a recommendation that within a specified period the respondent should take specified steps for the purpose of removing or reducing the adverse effect of any matter to which the proceedings relate, either on the complainant, or more generally with regard to the wider workforce.

According to the Code of Practice on Employment (EHRC 2011a), provided that the employee has sufficient continuous employment at the date of termination, a dismissal that amounts to a breach of the Act will almost inevitably be an unfair dismissal as well. In such cases, a person can make a claim for unfair dismissal at the same time as a discrimination claim.[30] The Code provides the following example:

> An employee who has worked with his employer for five years provides a witness statement in support of a colleague who has raised a grievance about homophobic bullying at work. The employer rejects the grievance and a subsequent appeal. A few months later the employer needs to make redundancies. The employer selects the employee for redundancy because he is viewed as 'difficult' and not a 'team player' because of the support he gave to his colleague in the grievance. It is likely that the redundancy would amount to unlawful victimisation and also be an unfair dismissal.

An employment tribunal also has jurisdiction to consider claims relating to equality clauses, including claims related to pregnancy and maternity equality. This can include jurisdiction to decide on an application as to the rights of an employer and a worker in a dispute about the effects of an equality clause or rule. A person making this request or bringing a complaint about a breach of the equality rule must do so within six months of the end of the employment contract in a standard case. It can be longer in cases of incapacity or concealment of information by the employer.

---

30 Para 10.16 Code of Practice on Employment.

3.8 Liability of employers and employees

According to section 109(1) Equality Act 2010:

> Anything done by a person (A) in the course of A's employment must be treated as also done by the employer.

Thus the employer is liable for any acts done by the employee in the course of their employment and section 109(2) provides that it does not matter whether this has been done with the employer's knowledge or approval.

Sometimes it is difficult to decide whether an act has taken place during the course of employment, especially if it takes place outside normal office hours. The Court of Appeal stated in *Jones v Tower Boot Co Ltd* [31] that the words ought to be given their everyday meaning. The following cases concerned contrasting outside hours events, first in *Sidhu*,[32] where a racially motivated assault took place at a 'family day out' organised by the employers and, second, in *Stubbs*,[33] where an incident of inappropriate sexual behaviour took place during a leaving party. Whether a person was, or was not, on duty and whether the events occurred on the employer's premises are two indicators that need to be considered. In the *Jones* case the day out was held to be outside the course of employment, whilst in *Stubbs* it was held that that the two police officers could not have been merely socialising outside their normal course of employment.[34]

The employer does have a defence if they can show they 'took all reasonable steps' to prevent the employee from carrying out the act. The employer needs to show that they have taken steps to prevent the employee from carrying out the act or other acts of a similar description.

3.9 Relationships that have come to an end

Section 108(1) and (2) of the Equality Act 2010 makes it unlawful for employers to discriminate against or harass employees after a relationship has ended. An employer will be liable for acts of discrimination or harassment arising out of the work relationship and which are closely connected to it. The phrase 'closely connected to it' is not defined by the Act. The protection includes the failure to make reasonable adjustments for a person with a disability.[35] An employee will be able to enforce their rights as if the relationship had not ended.[36]

3.10 Aiding contraventions

Section 112(1) of the Equality Act 2010 provides that A must not knowingly help another (B) to do anything that contravenes the provisions of the Act in relation to work and other matters (a basic contravention), although it is not a contravention if A relies on a statement by B that the help that is being given does not contravene the Act and it is reasonable for A to do so.[37] The making of such a statement by B is an offence if it is made knowingly or recklessly and is false or misleading.[38]

---

31 [1997] IRLR 168 CA.
32 *Sidhu v Aerospace Composite Technology Ltd* [2000] IRLR 602 CA.
33 *Chief Constable of the Lincolnshire Police v Stubbs* [1999] IRLR 81.
34 See also *Waters v Commissioner of Police of the Metropolis* [2000] IRLR 720 and *Lister v Hesley Hall Ltd* [2001] IRLR 472.
35 Section 108(4) Equality Act 2010.
36 Section 108(3) Equality Act 2010.
37 Section 112(2) Equality Act 2010.
38 Section 112 (3) Equality Act 2010.

The meaning of 'knowingly aided' has been considered by the courts and the House of Lords has said that the word 'aid' did not have any special or technical meaning.[39] An extreme example can be seen in *Gilbank v Miles*,[40] where a pregnant hairdresser was subject to a campaign of bullying and discrimination that led to the salon manager being made jointly and severally liable with the company employer as she had helped create the growth of a discriminatory culture. In *Hallam v Cheltenham Borough Council*[41] the police had concerns about a wedding reception that was to be held at a council-owned hall. The council were found to have committed racial discrimination by imposing new contractual conditions because the hirer of the hall was of Romany origin. One issue was whether the police had knowingly aided the council in this discriminatory act. The House of Lords held that each situation should be looked at on its merits. In this case the police officers had not been a party to, nor had they been involved in, the council's decision.

3.11 Contracts

A term of a contract is unenforceable if it promotes or provides for treatment that is prohibited by the Act.[42] According to the Code of Practice on Employment para 10.64, this will not stop a person relying on the unenforceable term to get any benefit to which they are entitled. Section 144(1) of the Equality Act 2010 also provides that a term of a contract that tries to limit or exclude a provision of the Act is unenforceable. This does not prevent the parties coming to an agreement to settle a claim via a compromise agreement with the help of an ACAS official.[43]

3.12 The Enterprise and Regulatory Reform Act 2013

This Act[44] repeals some provisions of the Equality Act 2010 with which the Coalition government strongly disagreed. In section 40(2)–(4) of the Equality Act 2010 provision had been made for employers to be liable for harassment that had taken place against an employee by a third party. The condition, contained in section 40(3), was that the employer knew of the harassment and that it had taken place on more than one occasion and had failed to take reasonable steps to prevent it. An example given (see above) was harassment of a shop worker by a customer. A further example given by the Equality and Human Rights Commission Employment Code of Practice was:

> An employer is aware that a female employee working in her bar has been sexually harassed on two separate occasions by different customers. The employer fails to take any action and the employee experiences further harassment by yet another customer. The employer is likely to be liable for the further act of harassment.

The government had consulted on its proposal to repeal this provision and decided to press ahead, despite the fact that the majority of responses were in favour of keeping the provision. The government's own summary[45] stated that:

---

39 *Anyanwu and Ebuzoeme v South Bank Students Union and South Bank University* [2001] IRLR 305.
40 [2006] IRLR 538.
41 [2001] IRLR 312 HL.
42 Section 142(1) Equality Act 2010.
43 Section 144(4) Equality Act 2010.
44 At the time of writing, the Enterprise and Regulatory Reform Bill had not passed all its stages in Parliament, but here it is assumed that this has now taken place.
45 http://www.homeoffice.gov.uk/publications/about-us/consultations/third-party-harassment/ (last accessed 17 January 2013).

We received 80 responses, of which 16 (20 per cent) agreed our proposal for repeal and 57 (71 per cent) opposed it. Responses which agreed with the proposals came mostly from individual public, private and not-for-profit sector employers and business organisations. All business representative organisations supported repeal. Responses which disagreed with our proposal were mainly on behalf of public sector employers, unions and equality lobby groups.

Despite this the provision was repealed by the Enterprise and Regulatory Reform Act, section 57.

In addition, section 58 of the Enterprise and Regulatory Reform Act repealed section 138 of the Equality Act 2010 concerned with obtaining information from an employer to assist in tribunal proceedings. Thus a worker who had a complaint under the Equality Act could have requested information about the reason for the treatment that was the subject of the complaint. This procedure was intended to be in addition to her means of obtaining information under employment tribunal rules. The Employment Code of Practice gave an example:

A lesbian employee who suspects that she has been denied a promotion because of her sexual orientation could use the procedure to ask her employer about their decision not to promote her. This information could support her suspicion or resolve her concerns.

This was a powerful means of enabling the employee to find out further information and to decide whether to proceed with a complaint, but the government decided against it and included it in its list of measures to be repealed.

3.13 Summary

It can be said that the Equality Act 2010 is a great achievement. It managed to replace about one hundred other pieces of statute and regulation and combine them into one large piece of legislation, bringing with it some uniformity of approach. Nevertheless, it still contains nine explicit protected characteristics and the option of a tenth remains open, namely that of caste. It is questionable whether such a closed list can provide protection against all discrimination that takes place at work and elsewhere. Alternative approaches suggested have consisted of either having an open-ended list such as that contained in Article 14 of the European Convention on Human Rights, or replacing all the possible protected characteristics with an overarching one such as 'human dignity', thus giving protection against all discriminatory acts that affect this.

Another major issue is that of equal pay between men and women. There is still a substantial gender gap, even though we have had an Equal Pay Act for almost 40 years. Much litigation continues in the courts on this subject. The question, therefore, is whether we should be doing something much more positive, such as regular equal pay audits, to expose those employers who continue to treat women as second-class workers. The Equality Act 2010 has taken some steps forward in this regard, but pressure from employers seems to limit the government's willingness to act in a positive way.

Chapter 4

Age and Ageism

Chapter Contents

4.1 Introduction

Age is a really interesting protected characteristic because everyone has an age and so the whole population is at risk of ageism or some form of related discrimination. It is also not a static characteristic, because most people will 'progress' through various stages from youth to old age. The risk of less favourable treatment will vary according to the age at which one finds oneself. It appears that, in terms of employment, it is the youngest and the oldest age groups that are at most risk of discrimination on the grounds of their chronological age.

Because everyone has an age, there is also perhaps a significant risk of multiple discrimination, so that age is added to at least one other protected characteristic to increase the possibility of disadvantage. For example, although the unemployment rates for young people (16–24 year olds) in the UK are very high, the unemployment rates for young black people are significantly higher than those for young white people. According to figures from the government Office for National Statistics, the unemployment rate for young people in 2011 stood at 21.9%; the same figure was 20.8% for young white people compared to some 47.4% for young black people. This suggests that the latter group suffered because of both their age and their colour or ethnic origin.[1]

It is also interesting to speculate as to why the UK has legislation on age discrimination at all. The USA adopted the Age Discrimination in Employment Act in 1967 on the coat-tails of the civil rights legislation on race and sex. In the UK and the EU the experience is much more recent. Successive UK governments rejected the idea of legislation on age discrimination[2] and even introduced a voluntary code of practice on age in 1999.[3] The Framework Directive, including age, was, of course, adopted in 2000. Most countries were allowed three years to transpose it into national law, but there was the possibility of asking for an extension of a further three years, which the UK took. Thus the UK finally implemented the Directive in 2006 when it adopted the Employment Equality (Age) Regulations.[4] Most of these Regulations have now been incorporated into the Equality Act 2010.

The simple answer as to why we have age regulation in the UK is that we were obliged to implement an EC Directive on the subject. The debate is more complicated, however. There are perhaps two important arguments for introducing measures to combat age discrimination in employment. These are, first, one that is related to demographic trends and, second, one that is related to the right to equal treatment as a human right. Demographic trends connected to the ageing of the population are a powerful argument for action and these trends are considered further below. This demographic justification, however, contrasts with the equality argument, which is that discrimination on the grounds of age is just as wrong as discrimination on the grounds of race or sex. It should really not be related to discussions about the ageing of the population because the principle of non-discrimination should apply anyway. It is simply wrong to treat a person differently because of a stereotypical view that assumes that people of a certain chronological age have certain common attributes. It is as wrong as applying racial stereotypes to people of different colours or ethnic origins. A debate about a demographic justification as opposed to an equality justification is not purely an academic debate. It might, for example, be more feasible to justify exceptions to equal treatment with regard to age if the reason for having the rule in the first place was justified by demography rather than by a need to apply the principle of equality. We shall see

---

1 Office for National Statistics at http://www.ons.gov.uk/ons/publications/re-reference-tables.html?edition=tcm%3A77–260216 (last accessed March 2012).

2 In 1998, for example, a backbench Member of Parliament, Ms Linda Perham MP, introduced the Employment (Age Discrimination in Advertising) Bill 1998. This received its second reading in February 1998. It failed to make any progress because it did not receive the support of the government and was the last of a long line of such Bills introduced to make unlawful the use of age limits in recruitment advertising or recruitment and selection.

3 Code of Practice for Age Diversity in Employment.

4 SI 2006/1031.

later in this chapter that the courts, including the Court of Justice of the European Union (CJEU), have accepted the less favourable treatment of older workers in favour of other age groups in contradiction of any general principles of equality, for example.

4.2 Population ageing

The population of the world is ageing rapidly (UN Department of Economic and Social Affairs Population Division 2002). At the beginning of the twenty-first century the number of older people (those aged 60 plus) was approximately 600 million. This figure is three times that of 50 years earlier. By 2050 this figure is expected to triple again to almost two billion people. Also by 2050 the median age will have increased from 26 years at the beginning of the century to 36 years, with Niger predicted to be the youngest country with a median age of 20 years and Spain the oldest with a median age of 55 years. The reasons for this are generally a mixture of lower fertility rates, that is a reduction in the number of children being born, combined with an increase in longevity – people are living longer.[5]

The usual measure of fertility is the 'total fertility rate' (TFR). This is a measure of the mean number of live children born to a woman during her lifetime. The 'replacement' rate, that is the total fertility rate needed in order to keep the population the same size, is 2.1. Even though the TFR has increased in the EU in recent years, it is still below the replacement level in most Member States. Table 4.1 illustrates the TFR for a number of countries.[6]

Another development in assessing fertility rates is that women have also been having families at a later age.

In contrast to this, the population is living longer with a consequent increase in the number and proportion of older people. This is amply illustrated in Table 4.2, which shows the increase in life expectancy for the population in the same countries.

How this increase in life expectancy combined with a population living longer manifests itself in the population structure can be seen from Table 4.3.

Thus we can see that in all countries the proportion of the population aged 19 and under has decreased whilst that of the population aged 65 plus has increased. Indeed, in Germany and Italy there is a greater proportion of people aged 65 plus than those aged under 20 years. This clearly has

Table 4.1 Total fertility rate in selected EU Member States

Country	1980	1990	2000	2003	2009
France	1.95	1.78	1.87	1.87	1.98
Germany	–	–	1.38	1.34	1.36
Italy	1.64	1.33	1.26	1.29	1.42
Spain	2.20	1.36	1.23	1.31	1.40
UK	1.90	1.83	1.64	1.71	1.96
EU27	–	–	–	1.47	1.60

---

5 I am sure that this is an oversimplification of the causes of demographic change, but it seems enough for our purposes.
6 Eurostat (2011). Tables 4.2 and 4.3 are also derived from this publication.

Table 4.2 Life expectancy at birth by sex

| | Men | | Women | |
Country	1993	2009	1993	2009
France	73.4	78.0	81.7	85.0
Germany	72.8	77.8	79.4	82.8
Italy	74.6	79.1	81.0	84.5
Spain	74.1	78.7	81.4	84.9
UK	73.5	77.8	78.9	81.9
EU27	–	76.4	–	82.4

Table 4.3 Population structure by age group (%)

| | 0–19 | | 20–64 | | 65 plus | |
Country	1990	2010	1990	2010	1990	2010
France	27.8	24.4	58.3	58.8	13.9	16.8
Germany	21.8	18.8	63.3	60.6	14.9	20.7
Italy	24.5	19.0	60.8	60.8	14.7	20.2
Spain	28.8	19.8	57.8	63.3	13.4	16.8
UK	25.9	23.9	58.4	59.8	15.7	16.3
EU27	26.7	21.3	59.5	61.3	13.7	17.4

significance for the labour market and for the provision of other services such as health care and social care.

4.3 Attitudes to age

Age discrimination is a manifestation of ageism, which is about having an essentially negative image of older people. A UN report defined ageism as something that 'reinforces a negative image of older persons as dependent people with declines in intellect, cognitive and physical performance . . . older persons are often perceived as a burden, a drain on resources, and persons in need of care' (United Nations 2009). The word 'ageism' was first used by Robert Butler MD in 1969. Butler wrote a short article (1969) about the strongly negative reaction of white, affluent, middle-class residents to a proposal for a public housing project for the 'elderly poor' in their district. He described ageism as 'prejudice by one age group against other age groups'.

Attitudes to Age in Britain 2010/11 is a useful piece of research carried out for the Department of Work and Pensions (Sweiry and Willits 2012). Its research found that about 20% of survey respondents did not view age discrimination as serious whilst some 36% regarded it as very serious. Interestingly, younger age cohorts reported that age discrimination was more serious than older cohorts. Some 47% of those aged under 25 years said it was very serious compared with just 24% of those aged 65–79 years. The research also found that those under the age of 25 years reported as being twice as likely to be on the receiving end of age discrimination as those of other age groups. Generally stereotypical attitudes on the basis of age were common, with older people being reported as more friendly and having higher moral standards than the young. An example of stereotypes being associated with age can be found in the work of Judy McGregor with New Zealand employers. Her survey of employers (McGregor 2002) found that older workers were regarded as being more reliable, more loyal, more committed and less likely to leave than younger workers. They were also more likely to resist change and have problems with technology. This is illustrated by Table 4.4.

It is astonishing that anyone was willing to answer such questions. The issue is not whether any of the stereotypes are correct, but whether it is actually possible to assume that whole age cohorts are likely to have particular characteristics. It is the adoption and use of such stereotypical views that leads to age discrimination. The same survey asked employers to attribute characteristics to different age groups, and the 45 and over age group did not do so well. It scored highly in having the characteristics of leadership, strong work ethic and loyalty, but not so well in others. Young workers similarly faced prejudice based upon stereotypes. Their strengths lie in computer experience and enthusiasm, but they, according to this survey, were unlikely to have leadership qualities or a strong work ethic.

Age discrimination also takes place outside the labour market and one survey gave some examples where it has been suggested that discrimination (outside employment) takes place against older people.[7] These included car insurance, travel insurance, loans and mortgages, allowances for the disabled, social inclusion such as the lack of public toilets and seating, health care, education and transport.[8]

Table 4.4 New Zealand survey of age characteristics

Older workers are more likely to:	Agree %	Neither %	Disagree %
Be reliable	83.6	11.3	5.3
Be loyal	81.2	16.0	2.9
Be committed to the job	65.9	18.5	5.6
Be willing to stay longer in the job	61.6	32.2	6.8
Resist change	60.1	22.8	17.1
Have problems with technology	55.4	28.4	16.2
Be productive	52.5	37.4	10.1
Be less flexible	39.3	33.4	27.3
Be less willing to train	32.5	36.5	30.9
Be less promotable	32.4	41.0	26.6
Be away sick	7.1	36.8	56.2
Have lower expectations	31.3	33.6	35.0
Be less creative	22.4	43.8	33.9

---

7 Taken from Help the Aged Policy Statement on Age Discrimination in Facilities, Goods and Services (2007).
8 For a fuller analysis see Sargeant 2011a.

4.4 The Framework Directive

We considered the Directive[9] fully in Chapter 2. Article 2 provides that discrimination means direct discrimination, indirect discrimination and harassment, and these will be considered further below. Article 4.1 provides a possible exception for 'occupational requirements'. It may therefore be possible to justify an exception in relation to age if the difference in treatment is 'by reason of the nature of the particular occupational activities concerned or of the context in which they are carried out, [and] such a characteristic constitutes a genuine and determining occupational requirement, provided that the objective is legitimate and the requirement is proportionate'. Thus it is possible to objectively justify an occupational requirement for having someone of a particular age. The test is likely to be strictly interpreted by the courts.

Article 6 of the Directive is headed 'Justification of differences of treatment on the grounds of age' and has the effect of weakening the impact of the Directive in tackling age discrimination. It is worth citing the whole of Article 6.1:

> Notwithstanding Article 2(2), Member States may provide that differences of treatment on grounds of age shall not constitute discrimination, if, within the context of national law, they are objectively and reasonably justified by a legitimate aim, including legitimate employment policy, labour market and vocational training objectives, and if the means of achieving that aim are appropriate and necessary.
>
> Such differences of treatment may include, among others:
>
> (a) the setting of special conditions on access to employment and vocational training, employment and occupation, including dismissal and remuneration conditions, for young people, older workers and persons with caring responsibilities in order to promote their vocational integration or ensure their protection;
>
> (b) the fixing of minimum conditions of age, professional experience or seniority in service for access to employment or to certain advantages linked to employment;
>
> (c) the fixing of a maximum age for recruitment which is based on the training requirements of the post in question or the need for a reasonable period of employment before retirement.

Article 2(2) is concerned with direct and indirect discrimination and allows there to be justification for such discrimination. It is strange to state that differences of treatment do not constitute discrimination. These differences may, in fact, constitute discrimination, but what the Directive is saying is that the result is permissible discrimination. One example might be the recruitment of holiday representatives for holidays aimed at a particular age group. The employer might prefer the representatives to be of the same age group as the tourists. The recruitment of a certain age group might be objectively justifiable. It would be still be age discrimination but, possibly, permissible age discrimination.

It is important to note that it is possible to justify direct discrimination as well as indirect discrimination. Article 2.2(b) already makes it possible to justify indirect discrimination for all the grounds listed in the Directive, but Article 6 then takes this further with regard to age and allows justification for direct discrimination as well. This is the only ground for which this is allowed. It is reflected in the Equality Act 2010, which permits justification for direct age discrimination but not for any of the other characteristics. It does not appear clear why this should be the case, except

---

9 Council Directive 2000/78/EC establishing a general framework for equal treatment in employment and occupation.

perhaps that there are likely to be numerous instances where age-related rules, for example concerning young people, are likely to be justifiable. Perhaps allowing this exception was preferable to actually identifying those specific situations where it might be possible.

The second important issue to note is that this Article defines legitimate aims as including 'legitimate employment policy, labour market and vocational training objectives'. The list of justifiable differences is further expanded in (a), (b) and (c). As we shall see when we consider the decisions of the courts, the use of Article 6 and its broad definition of what constitutes a legitimate aim have permitted a number of exceptions to the principle of non-discrimination with regard to age.

The justification for an exception requires proportionality in the means of achieving the legitimate objective. A good example of European Court of Justice case law on this aspect can be found in the case of *Werner Mangold*.[10] The Court of Justice considered a situation where German law allowed for the employer to conclude, without restriction, fixed-term contracts of employment with employees over the age of 52 years.[11] According to the national government, the purpose of the German legislation was to encourage the vocational integration of unemployed workers. The Court agreed that such a purpose could be 'objectively and reasonably' justified. The question then was whether the means to achieving this legitimate objective were 'appropriate and necessary'. The problem was that the national legislation applied to all people over the age of 53 years and not just to those who were unemployed. The Court concluded:

> In so far as such legislation takes the age of the worker concerned as the only criterion for the application of a fixed-term contract of employment, when it has not shown that fixing an age threshold, as such, regardless of any other consideration linked to the structure of the labour market in question or the personal situation of the person concerned, is objectively necessary to the attainment of the objective pursued. Observance of the principle of proportionality requires every derogation from an individual right to reconcile, so far as is possible, the requirements of the principle of equal treatment with those of the aim pursued.

Thus it was on the grounds of proportionality that the Court held the measure to be not in accord with the Directive and it seems difficult to disagree with that conclusion. Taking away the employment protection rights from all employed workers over the age of 52 years was not appropriate and necessary when introducing a measure to help unemployed older workers. The principle of weakening employee protection in order to help their employability is an issue that needs to be considered seriously and has occurred in other cases at the CJEU (see below).

4.5 Young workers

The provisions of the Equality Act 2010 and the Framework Directive apply to all those at work. Thus, in relation to age, the protection is offered to younger as well as older people. Although it is older people who are mostly considered when one thinks of age discrimination, it is important not to ignore the other end of the age spectrum. Certainly the survey on *Attitudes to Age* 2010 (Sweiry and Willits 2012) mentioned above shows that many young people feel that they have been victims of age discrimination. One piece of evidence about discrimination that might be suffered by young workers is that which has been gathered about older workers. There are some similarities in

---

10 Case C-144/04 *Werner Mangold v Helm* [2006] IRLR 143.
11 This is, of course, a simplification, but the purpose here is to concentrate on the aspects of the decision concerning age discrimination.

experiences. According to a survey carried out by the Employers Forum on Age and Austin Knight[12] the most common ages for women to encounter ageism at work are 21 years and 40 years; for men the ages are 18 years and 50 years. The report states that just over half of respondents who felt that they had experienced ageism said that it was because they were seen as too young. The report 'reveals that one in four UK employees had been discriminated against at work because of their age – and it is clear that ageism does not discriminate. Young and old, male and female alike are affected'.[13]

Every stereotypical assumption about older people is also likely to be a stereotypical assumption about younger people. When, for example, an employer states that older people are more reliable, the employer is also saying that younger people are less reliable. Taylor and Walker's 1994 survey of 500 companies illustrate this. Figures such as the 36 per cent who thought that older workers were more cautious, the 40 per cent who thought that they could not adapt to new technology and the 38 per cent who thought that they would dislike taking orders from younger workers suggest that stereotypical attitudes remain strong. Yet what is important for our purposes here is that a statement such as one that suggests that older people are more cautious also implies that younger people are less cautious.

One way in which governments appear to try to make young workers more attractive to employers is to reduce their levels of employment protection. Here are some examples.

4.5.1 Austria

Hütter v TechnischeUniverisät Graz[14] was a case heard at the European Court of Justice. It concerned national legislation that excluded periods of employment completed before the age of 18 years from being taken into account when determining the remuneration of contractual public servants. The Austrian Law ('the VBG') did not permit any period of service before the age of 18 years to count towards any entitlements related to length of service. Mr Hütter completed an apprenticeship at the same time as another colleague, who was slightly older. When they were employed for three months after the apprenticeship, his colleague was therefore on a higher increment because of the amount of service that she had completed after the age of 18 years. A number of possible legitimate aims were put forward to justify this policy. One was that the measure promoted the integration of young people into the workforce because they were less expensive.[15]

4.5.2 France

In February 2006 the French government tried to introduce a new employment contract for people aged under 26 years called the Contrat Première Embauche (CPE). This contract allowed for a two-year period at its beginning when the contract could be terminated without justification by the employer and without any specific procedures to be followed by the employer. There was, of course, much protest against the proposals by trade unions and students, leading to the closure of many universities. Eventually the CPE was withdrawn by the government. The purpose of the new contract was to assist the employment prospects of young people and would likely to have been a legitimate aim. Yet it was openly discriminatory against those under the age of 26 years.[16]

---

12 See http://www.efa.org.uk/press_releases.php/140/ageism (last accessed 10 July 2011).
13 Ibid, note 24.
14 Case C-229/08 Hütter v Technische Universität Graz.
15 See Sargeant 2011b.
16 See Sargeant 2008. Chapter 4 written by Professor Sylvain Laloum is about France.

4.5.3 Germany

Seda Kücükdeveci v Swedex GmbH & Co. KG[17] was another case before the European Court of Justice. In this case the complainant had been dismissed after more than 10 years' employment since the age of 18 years. Paragraph 622 of the German Civil Code provided, amongst other matters, that 'in calculating the length of employment, periods prior to the completion of the employee's 25th year of age are not taken into account'. Her period of notice was therefore based upon the three years' service achieved after this age. The justification for this measure, according to the referring court, was the legislature's assessment that young workers generally react more easily and more rapidly to the loss of their jobs and greater flexibility can be demanded of them. A shorter notice period for younger workers also facilitates their recruitment by increasing the flexibility of personnel management.[18]

In the UK this is done through the manipulation of the national minimum wage, and this is discussed below.

4.6 Unlawful actions

As with most of the other protected characteristics, the Equality Act 2010 makes direct discrimination, indirect discrimination, harassment and victimisation on the characteristic of age unlawful. The Act substantially superseded the Equal Treatment in Employment (Age) Regulations 2006.[19] The main exception was in relation to Schedule 6 of the Regulations, which had provided for a procedure whereby workers could be given notice of retirement and could then request the right to continue working. The decision was left entirely to the employer, who was not required to give any reason for their decision. This procedure had been necessary because the government in 2006 had introduced a default retirement age. This was usually at the age of 65 years and meant that the employer could retire employees against their will. The default retirement age was abolished in 2011, thus rendering the process in schedule 6 redundant.

Schedule 5 of the Equality Act 2010 provides that a reference to a person who has, or shares, a particular protected characteristic is a reference to a person of a particular age group or persons of the same age group. So those affected can be individuals or groups of people of the same or similar age or who are part of an age range. Below we consider the subjects of direct and indirect discrimination and harassment in relation to age.

4.7 Direct and indirect discrimination

As mentioned above, age is the only protected characteristic where direct discrimination can be justified if it is for a legitimate aim and the means of achieving that aim are proportionate. It is also interesting because it is a characteristic where the comparator for the purposes of identifying direct discrimination is a person with the same characteristic, namely age. Direct discrimination occurs in this case when a person (A) discriminates against another (B) if, because of their age, A treats B less favourably than A treats or would treat others (derived from section 13(1) Equality Act 2010). It is therefore less favourable treatment compared to someone else of a different age. The most obvious example of direct discrimination would be to select one candidate for a job over another because the selected candidate was younger. *Wilkinson v Springwell Engineering*[20] is a good example of a claim for

---

17 Case C-555/07 *Seda Kücükdeveci v Swedex GmbH & Co. KG*.
18 See Sargeant 2008, which contains a chapter on Germany written by Dr Marlene Schmidt.
19 SI 2006/1031.
20 *Wilkinson v Springwell Engineering Ltd* ET case number 2507420/07.

direct discrimination that involved a young worker. Ms Wilkinson, who was 18 years old at the time of the termination of her employment, had worked at the company for less than three months. She had been introduced to the job by her aunt, who had previously carried it out. The employer claimed that she made too many errors and she was informed that she was too young for the job. This was disputed, but the tribunal judgment stated that 'it was possible to conclude that the basis upon which the respondents asserted they dismissed was based upon a stereotypical assumption founded on age'.

Of more importance perhaps is the case of *Seldon*.[21] The case concerned Mr Seldon, who was a senior partner in a law firm where the partnership deed contained a mandatory retirement clause. There was a requirement to retire from the partnership at the end of the year when the age of 65 was reached. When the time for retirement approached, Mr Seldon put forward a number of proposals to the partners that would enable him to continue working for another three years. The partners rejected this and offered him an ex gratia payment in recognition of his services. He told the firm that he was taking legal advice on a claim for age discrimination, after which the offer of the ex gratia payment was withdrawn. He began proceedings in March 2007 alleging direct age discrimination and victimisation (because of the withdrawal of the ex gratia payment offer). It took a further five years for the case to reach the Supreme Court.

The firm had put forward a number of what it claimed were legitimate aims to the Employment Tribunal, which accepted three of them relating to the retention of employees, workforce planning and allowing an older and less capable employee 'to leave without the need to justify the departure and damage dignity'. After a review of the case law at the Court of Justice of the EU, the Supreme Court concluded that two kinds of legitimate aims had been identified. These were inter-generational fairness and dignity. The first of these, which was stated as being 'comparatively uncontroversial', meant various things depending upon the particular circumstances of the employment. It could include facilitating access to employment for young people, but it could also mean enabling older people to remain in the workforce. It could also mean sharing limited opportunities to work in a particular profession fairly between the generations. The second general type of legitimate aim identified was dignity, which was an argument put forward by employers wanting the default retirement age established by the 2006 Age Regulations. It is concerned with avoiding the need to go through lengthy disciplinary and competence procedures when some older workers decline in performance and capacity. Retirement is seen as a way for older workers to exit the workforce with dignity rather than being dismissed for other reasons. There is an underlying issue here concerning the stereotyping of older workers, however.

In the event the court held that the legitimate aims needed to be justified not only by these social policy aims but also in relation to the individual situation of the employer, so that these general aims were applicable to the individual situation. It is possible to have a compulsory retirement age, but the complexities of having to justify the legitimate aim might be too much for many employers not wishing to get involved in further expense or litigation. For Mr Seldon the case continues. Although the Supreme Court ruled against him, saying that the employer had justified having a retirement age, the employer had not justified having the actual age of 65 years, rather than any other age. The court therefore returned the case to the Employment Tribunal to decide whether having a retirement age of 65 was a proportionate means of achieving the legitimate aims.

The case of *Palacios*[22] at the European Court of Justice concerned the question as to whether the prohibition on discrimination, in particular Article 2(1) of the Framework Directive, precluded a national law that allowed compulsory retirement clauses to be included in collective agreements.

21 *Seldon v Clarkson Wright and Jakes* [2012] UKSC 16.
22 Case C 411/05 *Félix Palacios de la Villa v Cortefiel Servicios SA* [2007] IRLR 989.

Mr Palacios was born on 3 February 1940 and had worked for Cortefiel since 1981. In accordance with the collective agreement he was dismissed when he reached the age of 65. The collective agreement stipulated that in 'the interests of promoting employment, it is agreed that the retirement age will be 65 years unless the worker concerned has not completed the qualifying period required for drawing the retirement pension, in which case the worker may continue in his employment until the completion of that period'. Mr Palacios claimed age discrimination because of his dismissal at age 65. The Court held that legislation requiring the termination of contracts at a certain age was to be regarded as imposing less favourable treatment for workers who reach that age when compared to workers of other ages. Unfortunately for Mr Palacios, the Court went on to judge that, in his case, there was a legitimate aim (reducing unemployment) and that retirement when one had one's full pension entitlement was a proportionate means of achieving this.

Indirect discrimination (section 19 of the Equality Act 2010) is the discriminatory effect of an otherwise neutral application of a provision, criterion or practice. One example in the government consultation on the Equality Act 2010 was that of a requirement for applicants for a courier job to have held a driving license for five years. There is no requirement given regarding age, but the condition of having a license for five years has the effect of indirectly discriminating against younger applicants. It is likely that a higher proportion of workers over the age of 40 years will meet the requirement compared to, say, those aged 25 years.

The case of *Homer v Chief Constable of West Yorkshire Police*[23] concerned a retired police officer who subsequently obtained a position as a legal adviser with the Police National Legal Database (PNLD). In 2005 the PNLD introduced a new grading structure with three 'thresholds' above the starting grade. In order to reach the third threshold it was necessary to have a law degree or 'similar fully completed'. In 2006 Mr Homer was regraded to the first and second thresholds, but not to the third, as he did not have a law degree, although he met the criteria in all other respects. The court stated that:

> Mr Homer would reach the age of 65 in February 2009. It was the expectation of both sides that he would retire then. If he were to undertake a law degree by part time study it would take him at least four years. The earliest he could have graduated would have been the summer of 2010, after his normal retirement date. In any event, it was unlikely that he would have obtained a place on a course starting in September 2006 if he only applied in May 2006.

In January 2008 the Employment Tribunal held that Mr Homer was indirectly discriminated against on grounds of age and that this was not objectively justified. However, the Employment Appeal Tribunal (EAT) held that he had not been indirectly discriminated against on grounds of age, although if he had been, it would not have been justified.

The Court of Appeal dismissed both his appeal and the respondent's cross-appeal, holding that Mr Homer had suffered because of his impending retirement and this was different from suffering because of his age. The Supreme Court reversed this decision and stated:

> A requirement which works to the comparative disadvantage of a person approaching compulsory retirement age is indirectly discriminatory on grounds of age. There is, as Lord Justice Maurice Kay acknowledged, 'unreality in differentiating between age and retirement'. Put simply, the reason for the disadvantage was that people in this age group did not have time to acquire a law degree. And the reason why they did not have time to acquire a law degree was that they were soon to reach the age of retirement. The resulting scrutiny may ultimately lead to the conclusion that the requirement can be justified. But if it cannot, then it can be modified so as to remove the disadvantage.

---

23 *Homer v Chief Constable of West Yorkshire Police* [2012] UKSC 15.

4.8 The Equality Act 2010

There are a number of interesting issues that arise from the implementation of the Equality Act in respect of age. The issues considered are those relating to length of service, the national minimum wage and retirement.

4.8.1 Length of service

Service-related pay and benefits may include salary scales, holiday entitlement, company cars, and so on, all or some of which may be related to length of service. Without some action, benefits linked to length of service may amount to age discrimination as younger people who have not served the necessary time required may suffer detriment. Paragraph 10(1) of schedule 9 provides that:

> It is not an age contravention for a person (A) to put a person (B) at a disadvantage when compared with another (C), in relation to the provision of a benefit, facility or service in so far as the disadvantage is because B has a shorter period of service than C.

Thus an employer may award benefits using length of service as the criterion for selecting who should benefit from the award. First, there is no need to justify any differences related to service of less than five years. Where service exceeds five years it needs to fulfil a business need of the undertaking.[24] What makes this exception even larger is the fact that the length of service can be the entire length of time (less absences) that an employee has worked for an employer or it can be the length of time worked at a particular level. Thus if a person were promoted to a new grade at regular intervals this period of five years could be considerably extended.[25]

Length of service[26] has also traditionally been a factor in deciding who should be made redundant and what benefit they should receive in compensation. This process may disadvantage younger employees as those with the longest service may be the last to be made redundant and, if they are, then they will receive greater benefits. The essential issue when there is a challenge to this apparent unfairness is whether redundancy schemes linked to length of service can be justified by having a legitimate aim achieved by means that are proportional.

Rolls Royce v Unite the Union[27] considered two collective agreements that had an agreed process to be used to choose who should be selected for redundancy. There were five criteria against which an individual could score between 4 and 24 points. In addition there was a length of service criterion that awarded 1 point for each year of continuous service. Thus older employees would have an important advantage over younger ones. The process, unless justified, would constitute age discrimination.

The subject of whether there can be a general exception to the need to justify using length of service, or seniority, as a criterion has been an issue in a number of cases at the European Court of Justice, particularly in equal pay cases where the use of such a criterion could involve less advantageous treatment of women. Generally the Court of Justice accepted that length of service was justifiable by saying that 'length of service goes hand in hand with experience, and experience generally enables the worker to perform his duties better'.[28] The Court of Appeal in *Rolls Royce* accepted that to reward long service in a redundancy selection process was an entirely legitimate and reasonable

---

24 Section 10(2) Schedule 9 Equality Act 2010.
25 Section 19(3) Schedule 9 Equality Act 2010.
26 For a more detailed analysis of this see Sargeant (2009a).
27 *Rolls Royce plc v Unite the Union* [2009] IRLR 576.
28 See, for example, Case C-17/05 *Cadman v Health and Safety Executive* [2006] IRLR 969.

employment policy in accordance with Article 6 of the Framework Directive. The legitimate aims were the reward of loyalty and the achievement of a stable workforce, and using the length of service criterion was a proportionate means of achieving that aim.[29]

4.8.2 The national minimum wage

There is also an exception concerning the national minimum wage so that employers can pay the lower rate for those under 21 and 18 years without it amounting to age discrimination.[30] The intention is to help younger workers to find jobs by making them more attractive to employers. One question is whether such a measure is a proportionate response to the problem. In *Mangold v Helm*[31] the European Court of Justice considered a German law that restricted the use of fixed-term contracts, but did not apply these restrictions to those aged 52 years and over. The aim of this measure was to make older workers more attractive to employers. The Court accepted that the purpose of this legislation was to help promote the vocational integration of unemployed older workers and that this was a 'legitimate public-interest objective'. However, not only does the objective need to be legitimate, but the means used to achieve the objective also need to be 'appropriate and necessary'. The problem with the German law was that it applied to all workers of 52 years and older, whether unemployed or not. The result was that a significant body of workers was permanently excluded from 'the benefit of stable employment' available to other workers. The Court held that this measure went beyond what was appropriate and necessary in order to attain the objective pursued. There must be an issue as to whether the same logic applies to the national minimum wage and young people and whether the application of a universal lower minimum wage for younger people is an appropriate and necessary response to the problem of youth unemployment.

4.8.3 Retirement

The Framework Directive does not say a great deal about retirement ages. Paragraph 14 of the Preamble states that the Directive shall be 'without prejudice to national provisions laying down retirement ages'. Article 6.2 allows for the fixing of ages for invalidity and retirement schemes, and the use of ages for actuarial calculations, without it constituting age discrimination. Article 8.2 provides that any measures implementing the Directive shall not lessen the protection against discrimination that already exists in the Member State.

In implementing the Directive, the United Kingdom adopted a default retirement age of 65 years. Retirement below the age of 65 years needed to be objectively justified and presumably this will be entirely possible and proper in some cases. Section 98 of the Employment Rights Act 1996 was amended to add another fair reason for dismissal, which was the 'retirement of the employee'. As a result it was possible to compulsorily retire workers at the age of 65 years without the employer risking actions for unfair dismissal or for age discrimination. This provision was challenged by the age NGO Age Concern[32] in the High Court.[33] Aspects of the case were referred to the European Court of Justice,[34] but the challenge was unsuccessful. In the event, in 2011 the government abolished the default retirement age,[35] so that any compulsory retirement that now takes place

---

29 Other cases that might be of interest with regard to this subject are *MacCulloch v ICI plc* [2008] IRLR 846 and *Loxley v BAE Systems (Munitions and Ordnance) Ltd* [2008] IRLR 853.

30 Para 11 Schedule 9 Equality Act 2010.

31 Case C-144/04 *Werner Mangold v Helm* [2006] IRLR 143.

32 Now Age UK.

33 R (on the application of *Age UK*) *v Secretary of State for Business Innovation and Skills* [2009] IRLR 1017.

34 Case C-388/07 R (on the application of the Incorporated Trustees of the National Council on Ageing) *v Secretary of State for Business, Enterprise and Regulatory Reform* [2009] IRLR 373.

35 The Employment Equality (Repeal of Retirement Age Provisions) Regulations 2011 SI 2011/1069.

would need to be justified by the employer as having a legitimate aim and that the means of achieving that aim (i.e. retirement) were appropriate and necessary. It is believed that this would only be possible in exceptional circumstances.

4.9 Summary

In this chapter we have considered some of the basic issues surrounding age discrimination, particularly at work, but it must be obvious that age equality is treated differently to the other protected characteristics. There are more opportunities to show exceptions for both direct and indirect discrimination, providing that there is a 'legitimate aim' and the means of achieving that aim are proportionate. Part of the problem is that age does not really seem to have been accepted as a human rights issue as have the other protected grounds. The justification for having measures concerning age is essentially an economic one. The population is ageing and the workforce is ageing, so unless some action is taken, the strain on the pensions systems will be too great and the burden on society of supporting this older population will be excessive. Tackling age discrimination in order to encourage workers to stay longer at work is seen as an important contribution to this. Much progress has been made with such reforms as ending the general mandatory retirement age and tackling ageism in various parts of society (see Chapter 1 with regard to the Health Service). The problem is that if there is an economic justification for such a measure, then it is easier to justify exceptions on economic grounds and the principle of non-discrimination can take second place.

Chapter 5

Disability

Chapter Contents

5.1 Introduction

There are over 11 million people in Great Britain with a disability covered by the Equality Act 2010, with about 5.2 million being of working age and about 0.8 million who are children.[1] This constitutes some 19 per cent of the working population. Only half of disabled people of working age are in work, compared to 80 per cent of the non-disabled population.[2] The prevalence of disability rises with age. Around 1 in 20 children are disabled, compared to around 1 in 7 adults of working age and almost 1 in 2 people over state pension age.

Conventionally there are two models of disability discrimination that are discussed. These are the medical and social models of disability. The medical model focuses on the disability and is concerned with treating that disability. There is a strong element of this in the UK legislation. The social model focuses on society and provides that the barriers to participation in society for disabled people are society's responsibility and an individual's disability is irrelevant. Thus the medical model is concerned with providing a wheelchair for a person with a disability that affects their mobility; the social model would be more concerned about making access to transport and buildings as wide as possible. If a person in a wheelchair cannot access a building, it is society's responsibility, not that of the disabled person.

There is much evidence that disabled people face discriminatory attitudes from those who are not disabled. A 2011 survey of people with disabilities[3] asked them the question: 'roughly how frequently do you experience discrimination against you as a disabled person?' The responses were that 19% stated that they experienced it every day, 30% every week and some 20% every month. Thus almost half the disabled people surveyed experienced discrimination on a weekly, or more frequent, basis; and over two-thirds experienced it at least once per month. The same survey also asked about which kinds of discrimination had been suffered by the respondents. The responses to this question are contained in Table 5.1.

Table 5.1 Types of discrimination suffered by people with disabilities

Discrimination	Proportion of disabled people experiencing this (%)
Not being served in a shop, bar or restaurant	25
Ignored by a taxi or a bus you were trying to hail	27
Person not talking directly to you	67
Person talking to you in a patronising way	74
Person being aggressive, hostile or calling names	37
Person assuming you do not work	42
Person not believing that you are disabled	54
Person refusing to make adjustments or do things differently	63
Staring	58
Other	21

---

1 Office for Disability Issues, information on the website of the Department for Work and Pensions: http://odi.dwp.gov.uk/docs/res/factsheets/disability-prevalence.pdf (last accessed March 2012).

2 From the website of the Disability Living Foundation: http://www.dlf.org.uk/content/key-facts (last accessed March 2012).

3 Survey on behalf of SCOPE carried out by COMRES. Available at: http://www.comres.co.uk/poll/8/scope-discrimination-survey-15-may-2011.htm (last accessed March 2012).

It is important to remember that one in five disabled persons suffer this discrimination on a daily basis. Many experience being patronised, not being talked to directly (does he take sugar?), being stared at or just people not being prepared to do things differently to take into account a disability. Some of the quotes from the respondents about their experiences are contained in the survey summary.[4] They include:

> I have had people shouting abuse in the street, like 'scrounger'. I have been attacked by a group of teenagers, who attempted to kick my stick away and knock me down. This happened in a busy shopping area and no one offered to help me afterwards.

> MS is sometimes invisible. I have had a cab driver yell at me for some time in front of my four-year-old for parking my car (in a disabled bay) legally whilst displaying my blue badge in front of the bank.

> I have been called scrounger, parasite, and a waste of space. My personal assistant was spat at for helping me recently in a local shop.

> I've been called names in the street and told to 'stop faking and get a f***ing job' while struggling to transfer to my wheelchair from the car.

> People have referred to my disability railcard as a 'cripple pass'.

A further question in the survey asked the disabled respondents the question: 'Do you feel that a stranger has ever acted in a hostile, aggressive or violent way towards you because you are a disabled person?' Somewhat alarmingly, over half (54 per cent) replied yes to this question.

5.2 The United Nations Convention

The United Nations Convention on the Rights of Persons with Disabilities and its Optional Protocol was adopted in December 2006 and entered into force on 3 May 2008. In the words of the United Nations,[5] it:

> follows decades of work by the United Nations to change attitudes and approaches to persons with disabilities. It takes to a new height the movement from viewing persons with disabilities as 'objects' of charity, medical treatment and social protection towards viewing persons with disabilities as 'subjects' with rights, who are capable of claiming those rights and making decisions for their lives based on their free and informed consent as well as being active members of society.

This shows the extent to which international attitudes have moved from the medical model of disability, which is focused on the individual's incapacities, to the social model, which focuses on the barriers erected by society against the full participation of people with disabilities. These models are discussed further below.

The Convention describes how rights apply to persons with disabilities and identifies where accommodations have to be made in order for persons with disabilities to exercise their rights. Article 3 of the Convention sets out the principles on which it is based:

---

4 See http://www.scope.org.uk/news/latest-attitudes-survey (last accessed March 2012).
5 The Convention 'home page' can be found at http://www.un.org/disabilities/default.asp?id=150 (last viewed March 2012).

The principles of the present Convention shall be:

(a)   Respect for inherent dignity, individual autonomy including the freedom to make one's own choices, and independence of persons;

(b)   Non-discrimination;

(c)   Full and effective participation and inclusion in society;

(d)   Respect for difference and acceptance of persons with disabilities as part of human diversity and humanity;

(e)   Equality of opportunity;

(f)   Accessibility;

(g)   Equality between men and women; and

(h)   Respect for the evolving capacities of children with disabilities and respect for the right of children with disabilities to preserve their identities.

These are powerful principles that show an intention to tackle the disadvantageous treatment of those with disabilities. Turning the words into reality is something that is much needed, as one can tell from the treatment of the disabled as described above. Signature states are required to take legislative and other measures to end discrimination and abuse of the human rights of people with disabilities. Article 5 is concerned with equality and non-discrimination and provides that states 'shall prohibit all discrimination on the basis of disability and guarantee to persons with disabilities equal and effective legal protection against discrimination on all grounds'. It also requires states to take appropriate action to ensure that reasonable accommodation is provided (see below).

5.3 The Equality Act 2010

The Framework Directive on Equal Treatment in Employment and Occupation included proposals to combat discrimination on the grounds of disability 'with a view to putting into effect in the Member States the principle of equal treatment'. In particular it provided (Article 5) that employers should have a duty of 'reasonable accommodation'. This means that employers are obliged to take steps, when needed, to ensure that a person with a disability could have access to, participate in, have advancement in and undergo training. The only possible exception to this duty, according to the Directive, is if this places a 'disproportionate burden' on the employer. Thus in certain circumstances the Directive permits positive discrimination in favour of the disabled employee or applicant.

The Disability Discrimination Act (DDA) 1995 was the first measure to outlaw discrimination against disabled people in the United Kingdom and included an obligation on the employer to make adjustments. The Act, which preceded the Framework Directive, gives disabled people rights in employment and other areas.

The Equality Act 2010 now precludes direct and indirect discrimination, harassment and victimisation in relation to disability. It is important to note that the Act provides for indirect discrimination. Section 15(1) also provides that a person discriminates against a disabled person if the disabled person is treated unfavourably because of something arising in consequence of his or her disability. Thus there is no requirement for a comparator and no need to show detriment. These provisions effectively reverse the decision in LB of Lewisham v Malcolm.[6] Malcolm, which had severely limited the opportunity to complain about unfavourable treatment, related to disability by requiring there to be a comparator who did not share the disability of the complainant. None of this applies,

---

6 [2008] IRLR 700.

however, if the employer did not know, or could not reasonably be expected to know, that an individual had a disability (section 15(2)).

5.4 The meaning of disability

Having looked at the sort of discrimination from which people with disabilities can suffer, we now move on to consider what is actually meant by the term disability. There are of course many types of disability. The government Office for Disability Issues (ODI) provides the breakdown and analysis of prevalence[7] shown in Table 5.2.

Many disabled people have more than one impairment.

There is a legal definition of disability contained in the Equality Act 2010. Section 6(1) of the Act provides that:

(1)   A person (P) has a disability if—

(a)   P has a physical or mental impairment, and

(b)   the impairment has a substantial and long-term adverse effect on P's ability to carry out normal day-to-day activities.

Thus the tests for whether a person has a disability are, first, that there must be a physical or mental impairment; second, that it must have a substantial adverse effect; third, that it must have a long-term adverse effect; and, finally, that this adverse effect must relate to the ability to carry out normal day-to-day activities. This is examined further below. A person who has had a disability in the past is also protected by the Act.[8]

5.4.1 Physical or mental impairment

The government Office for Disability Issues has produced Guidance on matters to be taken into account in determining questions relating to the definition of disability.[9] It states that the term mental or physical impairment should be given its everyday meaning.[10] It is not necessary to investigate the

Table 5.2 Prevalence of disability by impairment in Great Britain (millions)

Mobility	6.2
Lifting, carrying	5.9
Manual dexterity	2.6
Continence	1.5
Communication	2.1
Memory, concentration, learning	2.2
Recognising when in danger	0.7
Physical co-ordination	2.4
Other	3.7
All with at least one impairment	10.9

7 See note 1; figures are for 2009/10.

8 Section 6(4) Equality Act 2010.

9 Office for Disability Issues Equality Act 2010 Guidance, available at: http://www.equalityhumanrights.com/uploaded_files/ EqualityAct/odi_equality_act_guidance_may.pdf (last viewed in March 2012).

10 See, for example, *McNicol v Balfour Beatty* [2002] IRLR 71 where the Court of Appeal stated that the term 'impairment' should have its 'ordinary and natural meaning'.

cause of the impairment or for the impairment to have been the result of an illness. An example of this can be found in *Power v Panasonic UK Ltd*,[11] which concerned an area sales manager who had the area for which she was responsible expanded, following a reorganisation. She became ill and was eventually dismissed after a long period of absence. During her long absence she was both depressed and drinking heavily and the tribunal concerned itself with whether the drinking or the depression came first. However, the EAT stated that it was not necessary to consider how the impairment was caused. What was relevant was to discover whether the person had a disability within the meaning of the Act at the relevant time.

It is important to look at the effect of the impairment on the individual's ability to carry out day-to-day activities. The Guidance provides examples of this:

A woman is obese. Her obesity in itself is not an impairment, but it causes breathing and mobility difficulties which substantially adversely affect her ability to walk.

A man has a borderline moderate learning disability which has an adverse impact on his short-term memory and his levels of literacy and numeracy. For example, he cannot write any original material, as opposed to slowly copying existing text, and he cannot write his address from memory.

So it is the effect of these conditions, that is the obesity and the learning difficulties, that is important and not the underlying conditions.

Goodwin v The Patent Office[12] concerned a man who was dismissed from his post after complaints from female staff of disturbing behaviour. He was a paranoid schizophrenic. He gave evidence that he heard voices and that these interrupted his concentration. The Employment Tribunal held that he was not disabled in terms of the (then) Disability Discrimination Act 1995 because the effect of these hallucinations was not substantial in relation to his normal day-to-day activities. The EAT reversed this decision and held that Mr Goodwin was disabled and that the tribunal had failed to consider the effect of the applicant's disability on his regular activities. The applicant was unable to carry on normal day-to-day conversations with his colleagues and this was good evidence that his ability to concentrate and communicate had been significantly adversely affected.

Certain conditions are automatically considered as disabilities. These include the case of a severe disfigurement, where the Act provides that this should automatically be treated as meeting the definition of disability.[13] This appears, however, to be treated as a narrow exception. In *Cosgrove v Northern Ireland Ambulance Service*[14] the court stated that the impairment here related solely to a condition of disfigurement and not to a condition, one aspect of which was disfigurement. Mr Cosgrove had applied for a job with the ambulance service and was turned down because he had severe psoriasis. The court decided that he had been turned down not because of the disfigurement but because he would be at risk of infection and of infecting others in the role of ambulance person.

Other exceptions included in the Act as specific disabilities are cancer, HIV infection and multiple sclerosis.[15] Without this inclusion one might have the strange situation of a person with

---

11 [2003] IRLR 151.
12 [1999] IRLR 4.
13 Equality Act 2010 schedule 1 para 3; although tattoos and body piercing are excluded from the meaning of severe disfigurement.
14 [2007] IRLR 397.
15 Equality Act 2010 schedule 1 para 6.

one of these ailments not meeting the definition of disability because there would be periods when the impairment would not have interfered with an individual's ability to carry out their day-to-day activities.[16] The Act also provides that certain people can be deemed to meet the definition of a disability.[17] These include the blind, severely sight-impaired, sight-impaired or partially sighted persons as certified by a consultant ophthalmologist.

Some conditions are specifically excluded from meeting the definition of disability.[18] These include addictions to alcohol or tobacco (provided that they have not been caused by medical treatment or prescribed drugs), a tendency to set fires, to steal, to physical or sexual abuse of other persons, to exhibitionism and to voyeurism. Seasonal allergic rhinitis (hay fever) is also excluded.

5.4.2 Substantial adverse effect

According to section 212(1) Equality Act 2010 the word 'substantial' means 'more than minor or trivial'. The Guidance gives some examples, the first of which is to consider the time taken to carry out a normal day-to-day activity. The comparison should be with a person who does not have the impairment. Here is the example from the Guidance:

> A ten-year-old child has cerebral palsy. The effects include muscle stiffness, poor balance and uncoordinated movements. The child is still able to do most things for himself, but he gets tired very easily and it is harder for him to accomplish tasks like eating and drinking, washing, and getting dressed. He has the ability to carry out everyday activities such as these, but everything takes much longer compared to a child of a similar age who does not have cerebral palsy. This amounts to a substantial adverse effect.

A second indicator might be the way in which a person carries out a day-to-day activity. The Guidance gives this example:

> A person who has obsessive compulsive disorder (OCD) constantly checks and rechecks that electrical appliances are switched off and that the doors are locked when leaving home. A person without the disorder would not normally carry out these frequent checks. The need to constantly check and recheck has a substantial adverse effect.

Paterson v Commissioner of the Police[19] concerned the issue of dyslexia. A chief inspector had claimed that, as a consequence of discovering that he had dyslexia, he was disabled within the meaning of the DDA. The tribunal dismissed his claim stating that, although his dyslexia was a substantial disadvantage to him when taking his promotion exam, this was not a day-to-day activity. Any adverse effects of his impairment were minor, not substantial. This decision was changed by the EAT, who held that carrying out an exam or assessment was a day-to-day activity, as were reading and comprehension. The EAT held that the only proper way to decide whether an impairment was substantial was to consider how the activity was actually carried out and compare this to how the activity would be carried out if the individual were not suffering from the impairment. 'If that difference is more than the kind of difference one might expect taking a cross section of the population, then the effects are substantial.'[20]

---

16 This was the case with the Disability Discrimination Act 1995 until it was amended by the Disability Discrimination Act 2005.
17 Equality Act 2010 schedule 1 para 7.
18 The Equality Act 2010 (Disability) Regulations 2010 SI 2010/2128.
19 [2007] IRLR 763.
20 *Paterson v Commissioner of Police*, para 68.

Many disabilities are controlled by medication and a disabled person may be able to carry out their normal day-to-day activities whilst taking the medication. This does not stop the person being regarded as disabled, however. The person's ability to carry out these activities, according to the Equality Act 2010, is to be assessed as if he or she is not taking the medication. In other words the effect of an impairment is to be assessed as if there are no medical controls in place.[21] The exception to this is sight impairments that can be corrected by the wearing of spectacles.

In *SCA Packaging Ltd v Boyle*[22] the court stated that where someone is following a course of treatment on medical advice, in the absence of any indication to the contrary, an employer can assume that, without the treatment, the impairment is 'likely' to recur. Similarly if it had a substantial effect on the individual's day-to-day life before it was treated, the employer can also assume that, in the absence of any contra-indication, if it does recur, its effect will be substantial. Treatment can include counselling sessions. In *Kapadia v London Borough of Lambeth*[23] a person suffering a form of depression had such sessions, but the Employment Tribunal failed to find that the individual was disabled within the terms of the DDA 1995, despite uncontested supporting medical opinion. The EAT held that the Employment Tribunal had erred in doing so and had arrived at a judgment based on how the complainant seemed when giving evidence.

Progressive conditions are also assumed to have a substantial adverse effect on a person's ability to perform day-to-day activities, provided that this will eventually be the situation.[24] Thus if someone has a progressive condition such as dementia, then they will meet the definition even if at the time there is no effect. The condition is progressive and, eventually, the individual's abilities will be impaired. An example given in the Guidance is:

> A young boy aged 8 has been experiencing muscle cramps and some weakness. The effects are quite minor at present, but he has been diagnosed as having muscular dystrophy. Eventually it is expected that the resulting muscle weakness will cause substantial adverse effects on his ability to walk, run and climb stairs. Although there is no substantial adverse effect at present, muscular dystrophy is a progressive condition, and this child will still be entitled to the protection of the Act under the special provisions in Sch1, Para 8 of the Act if it can be shown that the effects are likely to become substantial.

5.4.3 Long-term adverse effect

Schedule 1, para 2(1) of the Equality Act 2010 defines a long-term impairment as one that has lasted 12 months, is likely to last at least 12 months, or is likely to last for the rest of the life of the person affected.

According to the ODI Guidance, 'the cumulative effects of related impairments should be taken into account when determining whether a person has experienced a long term effect.' Similarly the substantial adverse effect of an impairment that develops from another impairment should also be taken into account when deciding whether the effect has lasted for 12 months or longer. This was the situation in *Patel v Oldham Metropolitan Borough Council*.[25] This case concerned a primary school-teacher who suffered from a mild inflammation of the spinal cord. She then developed a secondary syndrome that affected the same parts of her body. She had a phased return to work, but then suffered an injury whilst restraining a pupil in a swimming lesson. This further aggravated her pain

---

21 Equality Act 2010 schedule 1 para 5.
22 [2009] IRLR 746.
23 [2000] IRLR 14.
24 Equality Act 2010 schedule 1 para 8.
25 [2010] IRLR 280.

and after a long period of further absence she was dismissed. The Employment Tribunal decided that she was not disabled because she suffered from two different impairments over two different periods lasting less than 12 months. The Employment Appeal Tribunal disagreed and remitted to the case for further consideration of whether one impairment arose out of the other, in which case they combined to last for more than 12 months and the teacher would therefore meet the legislation's definition of disability. The Guidance gives an example of when an impairment does not meet the criteria for long term:

> A woman has two discrete episodes of depression within a ten-month period. In month one she loses her job and has a period of depression lasting six weeks. In month nine she suffers a bereavement and has a further episode of depression lasting eight weeks. Even though she has experienced two episodes of depression she will not be covered by the Act. This is because, as at this stage, the effects of her impairment have not yet lasted more than 12 months after the first occurrence, and there is no evidence that these episodes are part of an underlying condition of depression which is likely to recur beyond the 12-month period.

5.4.4 Normal day-to-day activities

According to the Guidance, the Act does not define day-to-day activities because it is not possible to provide an exhaustive list. Generally these are activities that people do on a regular basis, such as 'shopping, reading and writing, having a conversation or using the telephone, watching television, getting washed and dressed, preparing and eating food, carrying out household tasks, walking and travelling by various forms of transport.' This will include the impairments that affect the individual's ability to carry out duties at work, particularly if they include these 'normal day to day activities'.[26] The term normal day-to-day activities does not mean the activities that are only those of an individual or a small group of individuals. Account needs to be taken of how 'normal' the activities are for a large number of people. There will also need to be consideration of how frequently the activity is carried out in order to assess how normal it is. On the other hand 'normal' does not mean something that is carried out by the majority of people. It might be an activity carried out by only one particular gender, so it might be normal but not done by the majority.[27] In *Ekpe v Commissioner of Police*[28] the claimant suffered from the wasting of some muscles in her right hand. She worked for the Metropolitan Police, who had moved her to a job that involved keyboard duties, which, she claimed, she could not do. Evidence was given that there was an adverse effect on her ability to do normal day-to-day activities such as carry heavy shopping, scrub pans, peel, grate, sew or put rollers in her hair. The Employment Tribunal decided that this was not a substantial effect and some of these were not normal activities because they were only carried out by women. The EAT stated, however, that normal meant anything that was not abnormal. The court held that because some activities like putting rollers in her hair or applying make-up were only done by women, this did not stop them being normal. To exclude activities that were usually only done by women or men as not being normal was plainly wrong.

The Guidance states that highly specialised activities are not to be considered normal even if they are a regular part of an individual's life. The example of a pianist is given:

> A woman plays the piano to a high standard, and often takes part in public performances. She has developed carpal tunnel syndrome in her wrists, an impairment that adversely affects

---

26 *Law Hospital NHS Trust v Rush* [2001] IRLR 611, where the work of a nurse was stated to include some normal day-to-day activities.
27 Paras D3 and D4 of the Guidance.
28 [2001] IRLR 605.

manual dexterity. She can continue to play the piano, but not to such a high standard, and she has to take frequent breaks to rest her arms. This would not of itself be an adverse effect on a normal day-to-day activity. However, as a result of her impairment she also finds it difficult to operate a computer keyboard and cannot use her PC to send emails or write letters. This is an adverse effect on a normal day-to-day activity.

Sometimes an impairment may not actually prevent someone from carrying some day-to-day activities, but there may still be a substantial adverse long-term effect. This can be where, for example, an impairment causes pain or fatigue to someone when carrying out these activities; or it may be where a medical practitioner has advised against carrying out one or more day-to-day activity.[29]

The Guidance also states that the definition of direct discrimination is broad enough to include those treated less favourably because of their association with someone who has the characteristic or because the victim is thought to have it. This is shown to be the case in *Coleman v Attridge Law*,[30] which interpreted European Community law as extending protection from discrimination to those associated with an individual with the characteristic, rather than to just the individual alone. In this case a mother of a child with a disability claimed successfully that she was protected by the Disability Discrimination Act 1995 even though she was not herself disabled. She had been obliged to take a lot of time off work to look after her child.

5.5 Duty to make adjustments

An important aspect for the protection of people with disabilities at work is the duty to make adjustments (section 20 Equality Act 2010).

This duty has three requirements:

- A requirement, where a provision, criterion or practice of A's puts a disabled person at a substantial disadvantage in relation to a relevant matter in comparison with persons who are not disabled, to take such steps as it is reasonable to have to take to avoid the disadvantage.
- A requirement, where a physical feature puts a disabled person at a substantial disadvantage in relation to a relevant matter in comparison with persons who are not disabled, to take such steps as it is reasonable to have to take to avoid the disadvantage.
- A requirement, where a disabled person would, but for the provision of an auxiliary aid, be put at a substantial disadvantage in relation to a relevant matter in comparison with persons who are not disabled, to take such steps as it is reasonable to have to take to provide the auxiliary aid.

A failure to comply with any of these three requirements is a failure to comply with the duty to make reasonable adjustments, which in turn amounts to discrimination against the disabled person in question (section 21).[31]

A failure to make reasonable adjustments over a period of time would almost be bound to lead to a breach of the implied term of trust and confidence, which would then entitle the employee to treat it as a repudiatory breach of contract. *Nottinghamshire County Council v Meikle*[32] concerned a local

---

29 Para D9 of the Guidance.
30 *Coleman v Attridge Law* [2008] IRLR 722.
31 Schedule 8 of the Act expands further on the duty.
32 [2004] IRLR 703.

authority schoolteacher. Her vision deteriorated until she lost the sight in one eye and some vision in the other. She made a number of requests for adjustments, including to her classroom location, the amount of preparation time she was given and that notices and written materials should be enlarged. There were delays in responses from the employer and eventually Mrs Meikle resigned. The Court of Appeal agreed with her that the continuing failure of the local authority to deal with the disability discrimination amounted to a fundamental breach of contract and that she had been constructively dismissed.

It is the duty of the employer to take reasonable steps, in all the circumstances of the case, to prevent the provision, criterion, practice or feature from having that effect. This obligation applies in respect of applicants for employment as well as in respect of existing employees. There is, however, no obligation placed upon the employer if the employer does not know, or could not have reasonably been expected to know, that the applicant or employee had a disability.

The question of whether an employer had made sufficient arrangements in the light of their knowledge of an employee's disability is one of fact for the Employment Tribunal. *Ridout v TC Group*[33] concerned an applicant with a rare form of epilepsy, who may have been disadvantaged by the bright fluorescent lighting in the interview location. The EAT held that no reasonable employer could be expected to know, without being told, that the arrangements for the interview might place the applicant at a disadvantage. The EAT held that the DDA 1995:

> requires the tribunal to measure the extent of the duty, if any, against the assumed knowledge of the employer both as to the disability and its likelihood of causing the individual a substantial disadvantage in comparison with persons who are not disabled.

The extent of the adjustments needed is subject to a reasonableness test. This first requires an employer to carry out a proper assessment of what is needed to eliminate a disabled person's disadvantage. This might include a proper assessment of the individual's condition, the effect of the disability on her and her ability to perform the duties of the post and the steps that might be taken to reduce or remove the disadvantages to which she was subjected.[34] In deciding whether it is reasonable for an employer to have to take a particular step, regard may be had to the nature of the employer's activities and the size of the undertaking, as well as the extent to which the step would prevent the effect or barrier that existed and the practicability of taking the step in the first place. It may mean creating a new job for an individual, such as in *Southampton City College v Randall*,[35] where a reorganisation of work would have enabled the employer to create a new job for a lecturer whose voice had broken down. The employers were guilty of disability discrimination because they did not consider this option and others as possible reasonable adjustments.

A further example of the scope of the duty to make reasonable adjustments arose in *Archibald v Fife Council*.[36] This concerned an employee of Fife Council who was employed as a road sweeper. As a result of a complication during surgery she became virtually unable to walk and could no longer carry out the duties of a road sweeper. She could do sedentary work and the Council sent her on a number of computer and administration courses. Over the next few months she applied for over 100 jobs within the Council, but she always failed in a competitive interview situation. Eventually she was dismissed as the redeployment procedure was exhausted. The issue for the court was the limits of the duty to make reasonable adjustments. It was agreed that the DDA 1995 required some positive discrimination in favour of disabled people, but did this include finding them another job

33 [1998] IRLR 628.
34 *Mid Staffordshire General Hospitals NHS Trust v Cambridge* [2003] IRLR 566.
35 [2006] IRLR 18.
36 [2004] IRLR 651 CA.

if their disability stopped them from performing their current one? The court held that the DDA 1995, to the extent that the provisions of the Act required it, permitted and sometimes obliged employers to treat a disabled person more favourably than others. This may even require transferring them to a higher-level position without the need for a competitive interview.[37]

5.6 Positive action

Section 13(3) makes it clear that treating a person with a disability more favourably does not amount to discrimination against a person who does not have a disability.

Section 158 of the Equality Act 2010 allows generally for the taking of positive action measures to alleviate disadvantage suffered by people who share one of the protected characteristics. This can only be done if the participation of persons who share a particular protected characteristic is 'disproportionately low' (section 158(1)(c)). This provision is limited in that it will need to be interpreted in accordance with EU law and decisions of the European Court of Justice.

Section 159 then deals with positive action in relation to recruitment and promotion.

5.7 Recruitment

Section 60 of the Equality Act 2010 concerns enquiries about disability and health in recruitment. A person to whom an application for work is made (A) must not ask about the health of the applicant (B) before offering B work or where A is not in a position to offer work, before including B in a pool of applicants from whom A intends (when in a position to do so) to select a person to offer work. A contravention of this rule is enforceable as an unlawful act under Part 1 of the Equality Act 2006. A does not contravene a relevant disability provision merely by asking about B's health, but A's subsequent conduct in reliance on this information may be a contravention. There are a number of exceptions listed in section 60(6). Work has a wide meaning and includes employment and contract work (section 60(9)).

In order to limit the potential for discrimination, the Equality Act does specifically state that an employer must not ask about the health of an applicant, except for certain specific reasons, until the applicant has been either offered a job or has been included in a pool of successful applicants to be offered a job when a position arises (section 60(1)). The specific occasions when health enquiries can be made are:

1. establishing whether there is a need to make reasonable adjustments to enable the person with a disability to participate in the selection process;
2. establishing whether an applicant could participate in all parts of the selection process;
3. discovering whether an applicant could undertake a function that is specific to the job;
4. monitoring diversity in applicants;
5. supporting positive action for disabled people; and
6. enabling an employer to establish whether the applicant has a disability where there is an occupational requirement for someone with a disability.

Employers will therefore need to be careful not to have general health questions as part of the selection process unless it can be shown that they are for one of these specific purposes. If a candidate is

---

37 This was one of the problems for the employer. Most positions were at a higher level than that of a road sweeper and the local authority assumed that it had an obligation to make all promotion interviews competitive.

asked a question that cannot be shown to be for one of these purposes and they subsequently fail to get the job, they will be able to make a claim of direct disability discrimination.

It is also unlawful to discriminate against an employee in relation to the protected characteristics during a person's employment. This includes the individual's terms of employment, access to opportunities for promotion, training or transfer, dismissal and any other detriment (section 39(2)).

'Employment' covers engagement under a contract of service or a contract personally to execute any work or labour (section 83(1)). According to the Court of Appeal, the legislation contemplates (referring, of course, to pre-Equality Act legislation) a contract of which the dominant purpose is that the party contracting to provide services under it personally performs the work or labour that constitutes the subject matter of the contract.[38]

In *British Sugar plc v Kirker*[39] an individual selected for redundancy claimed that they had been discriminated against because of a visual impairment suffered since birth. The employers had carried out an assessment exercise in order to select those to be dismissed. This had consisted of marking employees against a set of factors. The complainant claimed that the marks attributed to them were the result of a subjective view arising out of the disability. The employee had scored 0 out of 10 for promotion potential and 0 for performance and competence. The EAT observed that such marks would indicate that the employee did not always achieve the required standard of performance and required close supervision. Yet the employee had never been criticised for poor performance and did not have any supervision. There was no need to consider the scores of other employees as the DDA 1995 did not require comparisons. It was clear that this individual had been undermarked by reason of their disability. The fact that many of the relevant events took place before the coming into force of the DDA 1995 did not stop the Employment Tribunal from looking at them in order to help draw inferences about the employer's conduct.[40]

5.8 Summary

In the measures concerning disability discrimination we can see a really strong act of positive discrimination, that is the duty to make reasonable adjustments. It is more difficult for people with disabilities to obtain work and keep it than it is for people without a disability. The duty to make adjustments places on employers a positive duty to take special measures in favour of the disabled employee, thus moving on slightly from the concept of formal equality to that of equality of opportunity. Of course the legislation has historically been focussed on the disabled person and measures to help them cope with an unequal society. A more positive model would be to focus the attention on society rather than the individual. It is society's fault that some of its citizens cannot access the transport system or do not stand an equal chance of finding employment as other people. The social model of disability encourages us to take this societal approach rather than the narrower medical approach of focussing on the disability.

---

38 See *Mirror Group Ltd v Gunning* [1986] IRLR 27 and *Percy v Church of Scotland* [2006] IRLR 195. Section 41 Equality Act 2010 makes discrimination against contract workers unlawful.
39 [1998] IRLR 624.
40 See also *Kent County Council v Mingo* [2000] IRLR 90 where a redeployment policy that gave preference to redundant or potentially redundant employees, in preference to those with a disability, amounted to discrimination in accordance with the DDA 1995.

Chapter 6

Pregnancy and Maternity

Chapter Contents

6.1 Introduction

One of the protected characteristics contained in the Equality Act 2010 is pregnancy and maternity. Section 18 provides:

(2) A person (A) discriminates against a woman if, in the protected period in relation to a pregnancy of hers, A treats her unfavourably —

    (a) because of the pregnancy, or
    (b) because of illness suffered by her as a result of it.

(3) A person (A) discriminates against a woman if A treats her unfavourably because she is on compulsory maternity leave.

(4) A person (A) discriminates against a woman if A treats her unfavourably because she is exercising or seeking to exercise, or has exercised or sought to exercise, the right to ordinary or additional maternity leave.

So a person discriminates against a woman if, in the protected period in relation to her pregnancy, she is treated unfavourably because of the pregnancy or any illness suffered by her as a result of it. This is different from most of the other protected characteristics, which require 'less favourable treatment'. In relation to disability and pregnancy/maternity the requirement is for 'unfavourable treatment'. Specifically this includes unfavourable treatment because the woman is on any kind of maternity leave or for exercising, seeking to exercise or having exercised her right to ordinary and additional maternity leave (section 18(4)). The reference to unfavourable treatment rather than less favourable treatment clearly shows that no comparator is required. The protected period begins when the pregnancy begins and ends, if the woman has the right to ordinary and additional maternity leave, at the end of the additional maternity leave period, or (if earlier) when she returns to work after the pregnancy. If she does not have that right, then it will stop at the end of two weeks beginning with the end of the pregnancy (section 18(6)).

The period during pregnancy and maternity leave has long been a specially protected one. The dismissal of a female worker on account of pregnancy can only affect women and therefore constitutes direct discrimination. Two early cases that clearly spelt out the protection were *Dekker* and *Webb v EMO*.[1]

In *Dekker* the complainant applied for the post of instructor at the training centre for young adults run by the VJV. She subsequently informed the committee dealing with the applications that she was three months' pregnant. The committee none the less put her name forward to the board of management of the VJV as the most suitable candidate for the job. Then VJV informed Mrs Dekker that she would not be appointed. The problem was that Mrs Dekker was already pregnant at the time of lodging her application and that, according to the information it had obtained, if the VJV were to employ her, the consequence would be that its insurer would not reimburse the daily benefits that the VJV would be obliged to pay her during her maternity leave. As a result, the VJV would be financially unable to employ a replacement during Mrs Dekker's absence and would thus be short-staffed. The Court of Justice took a clear view that:

an employer is in direct contravention of the principle of equal treatment . . . as regards access to employment, vocational training and promotion, and working conditions if he refuses to enter into a contract of employment with a female candidate whom he considers to be suitable for the job where such refusal is based on the possible adverse consequences for him of

---

1 Case C-177/88 *Dekker v Stichting Vormingscentrum voor Jonge Volwassen* [1991] IRLR 27 and Case C-32/93 *Webb v EMO Air Cargo (UK) Ltd* [1994] IRLR 482.

employing a pregnant woman, owing to rules on unfitness for work adopted by the public authorities which assimilate inability to work on account of pregnancy and confinement to inability to work on account of illness.

In *Webb* the company, EMO, employed about 16 workers. In June one of the four employees working in the import operations department, Mrs Stewart, found that she was pregnant. EMO decided not to wait until her departure on maternity leave before engaging a replacement whom Mrs Stewart could train during the six months prior to her going on leave. Mrs Webb was recruited with a view, initially, to replacing Mrs Stewart following a probationary period. However, it was envisaged that Mrs Webb would continue to work for EMO following Mrs Stewart's return. The documents before the court showed that Mrs Webb did not know she was pregnant when the employment contract was entered into.

Mrs Webb started work at EMO and two weeks later she thought that she might be pregnant. Her employer was informed of this indirectly. He then called her in to see him and informed her of his intention to dismiss her. Mrs Webb's pregnancy was confirmed a week later. She received a letter dismissing her in the following terms:

> You will recall that at your interview some four weeks ago you were told that the job for which you applied and were given had become available because of one of our employees becoming pregnant. Since you have only now told me that you are also pregnant I have no alternative other than to terminate your employment with our company.

The issue of course was whether it was permissible to consider the reasons why Ms Webb was recruited in the first place (to replace a pregnant employee) and whether this enabled her to be dismissed. The Court of Justice said that the reason for recruitment could not affect the decision concerning dismissal for reasons related to pregnancy. It stated that:

> In circumstances such as those of Mrs Webb, termination of a contract for an indefinite period on grounds of the woman's pregnancy cannot be justified by the fact that she is prevented, on a purely temporary basis, from performing the work for which she has been engaged.

6.2 Discrimination

Before it was absorbed into the Equality and Human Rights Commission, the Equal Opportunities Commission carried out a survey of pregnant women and work. It estimated that there were about 370,000 pregnant employees in any one year in the United Kingdom and concluded that around 30,000 women a year were sacked, made redundant or left their jobs due to pregnancy. The EOC survey also indicated that some 20 per cent lost out financially and some 5 per cent said that they were put under pressure to leave employment when they revealed their pregnancy. This is despite the fact that the period during pregnancy and maternity leave is a specially protected one. Prior to the Equality Act 2010, the dismissal of a female worker on account of pregnancy was, and still is, likely to constitute direct sex discrimination. This is because only women can become pregnant, so discrimination related to pregnancy and maternity is likely to be discrimination on the grounds of sex.

The key findings from the research were:[2]

- 7% of working women were either dismissed, made redundant, or left their jobs due to pregnancy discrimination;

---

2 Available at: http://www.eurofound.europa.eu/eiro/2005/05/feature/uk0505102f.htm (last accessed 17 January 2013).

- 45% of women who had worked while pregnant said they experienced 'tangible discrimination' such as denial of training opportunities and changes in job description;
- 21% had faced discrimination that may have led directly to financial loss;
- 5% were put under pressure to hand in their notice after announcing their pregnancy; and
- only half the women had a health and safety risk assessment carried out for their duties.

This does seem astonishing given the amount of protection that is, and has been, available to women who are pregnant or who have recently given birth.

6.3 The Pregnant Workers Directive

Article 2(a) of the Pregnant Workers Directive[3] defines a pregnant worker as a woman who informs her employer of her condition, in accordance with national laws and practice. Most Member States require the worker to inform her employer of her pregnancy, or of the fact that she has recently given birth or is breastfeeding, before the protective measures can begin.

Article 10(1) of the Directive provides that dismissal should be prohibited during the period from the beginning of pregnancy to the end of maternity leave, save in exceptional circumstances unrelated to the worker being pregnant, breastfeeding or having recently given birth. In *Brown v Rentokil Ltd*[4] the Court of Justice considered the dismissal of a female employee who was absent through most of her pregnancy and was dismissed under a provision of the contract of employment that allowed for dismissal after 26 weeks' continuous absence through sickness. The Court held that the Equal Treatment Directive 'precludes dismissal of a female worker at any time during her pregnancy for absences due to incapacity for work caused by an illness resulting from that pregnancy'.

The same strict approach is taken with situations where there are statutory restrictions on employing pregnant women. Not appointing or promoting them because of such a restriction might be considered to be sex discrimination. *Mahlberg v Land Mecklenburg-Vorpommern*[5] was a case where a pregnant woman was refused an appointment as an operating theatre nurse because German law banned pregnant women from being employed in areas where they would be exposed to dangerous substances. The financial loss that the employer might suffer because they could not employ the woman in the position for the duration of her pregnancy was not an acceptable reason for the unfavourable treatment.

In *P & O Ferries Ltd v Iverson*[6] a woman was stopped from going to sea once she reached week 28 of her pregnancy. Pregnancy was one of a number of lawful reasons for stopping an individual going to sea, but it was the only one for which there was no pay with this employer. All the other reasons, including sickness, resulted in suspension with pay. The fact that this was not available to pregnant women was held to be discriminatory.[7]

In *Mayr*[8] the Court of Justice considered the case of a woman undergoing *in vitro* fertilisation treatment. She was dismissed during the treatment period, but before the fertilised ovum was transferred to her uterus. That procedure was carried out three days after her dismissal. The Court

---

3 Directive 92/85/EEC on the introduction of measures to encourage improvements in the safety and health of pregnant workers and workers who have recently given birth or are breastfeeding.

4 Case C-394/96 [1998] IRLR 445.

5 Case C-207/98 [2000] IRLR 276.

6 [1999] ICR 1088.

7 See also British Airways (European Operations at Gatwick) Ltd v Moore and Botterill [2000] IRLR 296 for a similar approach in relation to air crew grounded because of pregnancy.

8 Case C-506/06 Mayr v Bäckerei und Konditorei Gerhard Flöckner OHG [2008] IRLR 387.

stated that the purpose of Article 10 was to protect pregnant women at the earliest possible moment from dismissal for reasons linked to the pregnancy. In the case of *in vitro* treatment, however, the protection commenced when the ovum was actually transferred. To do otherwise might give protection over a period of many years, as there can be a gap of years before the actual transfer.

There are various other protective measures contained in the Directive such as the need to carry out risk assessments and restrictions on working. The employer is required to complete an assessment of the risk of exposure to a non-exhaustive list of agents,[9] processes or working conditions and then to inform the worker or her representatives of the results and the measures intended to be taken concerning health and safety at work.[10] However, these measures should not go so far in their attempt to protect pregnant women that they breach the Equal Treatment Directive. In addition Article 7 of the Directive ensures that pregnant workers should not be obliged to carry out night work if it is detrimental to their health or safety. If there is such a risk, then the woman concerned should be moved to day work or given leave from work if day work is not possible.

Workers must be permitted to take a minimum of 14 weeks' continuous maternity leave with at least two weeks' compulsory leave taken before or after confinement.[11] In *Ulrich Hofmann v Barmer Ersatzkasse*[12] the Court of Justice was asked to consider a claim that the giving of leave to women alone did not accord with the terms of the Equal Treatment Directive. The claimant was a man who looked after a child whilst the mother returned to work as a teacher shortly after the birth. He was denied a claim for maternity benefit by the German social security service. The argument in the legal proceedings that followed was that the introduction of maternity leave was concerned not with the protection of the mother's health, but exclusively with the care that she gave to the child. If this argument was correct, it was said, then the leave should be available to either parent and become a form of parental leave. The Court rejected this approach and stated that the Equal Treatment Directive was not intended to 'settle questions concerned with the organisation of the family'. If national legislation had been only concerned with the care of the child, then it ought to be non-discriminatory. The Court held that maternity leave came within the scope of Article 2(3) of the Equal Treatment Directive, which 'seeks to protect a woman in connection with the effects of pregnancy and motherhood'. Thus maternity leave could legitimately be reserved for the mother, as it is only she who is likely to suffer from undesirable pressures to return to work prematurely.

6.4 Protection in the United Kingdom

Special measures to benefit pregnant women and women who have recently given birth were first introduced in the United Kingdom during the post-Second World War period. The National Insurance scheme, in 1948, introduced a maternity allowance for women contributors who gave up work to have a baby. This was paid for 13 weeks. The period was increased to 18 weeks in 1953. In 1975 the Employment Protection Act introduced six weeks' maternity pay for women who contributed to the Maternity Fund. This maternity pay equalled 90 per cent of normal weekly earnings less the amount of the maternity allowance. Maternity allowance and maternity pay were amalgamated in 1987 and became statutory maternity pay. This is paid by employers, who then recover their costs by deductions from their tax and national insurance contributions. Small employers can claim an additional amount in respect of such pay.

---

9 Article 4 Pregnant Workers Directive.
10 A failure to carry out a risk assessment amounts to sex discrimination: *Hardman v Mallon* [2002] ICR 510.
11 Article 8 Pregnant Workers Directive.
12 Case 184/83 *Ulrich Hofmann v Barmer Ersatzkasse* [1984] ECR 3047.

The Employment Protection Act 1975 also introduced the right to return to work for up to 29 weeks after confinement for women who had been employed for two years continuously with the same employer. In 1994 changes were made as a result of the Pregnant Workers Directive. These changes concerned the right for women to have at least 14 weeks' maternity leave, regardless of their length of service or hours of work. Two weeks of this were to be compulsory. They also concerned the payment to women of an 'adequate allowance' during their maternity leave period, equal at least to State rules on sickness benefit, although this could be limited to those with at least one year's continuous service.

The Equality Act contains specific provisions protecting women at work from discrimination because of pregnancy or maternity leave. There is also a separate statutory regime that sets out pregnant employee rights in relation to health and safety, time off, maternity leave and so on.

As with other protected characteristics the employer's motive is not relevant; it is not possible to justify discrimination. There is no need for a comparator because if a woman is treated unfavourably because of her pregnancy and maternity leave during the protected period, this is automatically discrimination on the grounds of pregnancy/maternity. Sometimes pregnant women will have to be treated more favourably than other workers, but men will not be able to claim sex discrimination if this happens.[13]

6.5 The Maternity and Parental Leave etc. Regulations 1999

The Maternity and Parental Leave etc. (MPL) Regulations 1999[14] provide for three types of maternity leave: ordinary maternity leave, compulsory maternity leave and additional maternity leave. These are periods of leave, before and after childbirth, to which a pregnant employee, or one who has recently given birth, is entitled. The dates of leave are calculated as being periods before or after the 'expected week of childbirth'. Regulation 2(1) of the MPL Regulations defines this as the week, beginning with midnight between Saturday and Sunday, in which it is expected that childbirth will occur. This regulation also defines childbirth as 'the birth of a living child or the birth of a child whether living or dead after 24 weeks of pregnancy'. This means, of course, that a woman who gives birth to a stillborn child after 24 weeks of pregnancy will be entitled to the same leave as a person who gave birth to a live child.

6.5.1 Compulsory maternity leave

An employee is obliged to take compulsory maternity leave. Section 72 of the Employment Rights Act (ERA) 1996 provides that an employer must not allow a woman who is entitled to ordinary maternity leave to work during the compulsory leave period. The compulsory leave period is for two weeks commencing with the day on which childbirth occurs.[15] These two weeks fall within the ordinary maternity leave period, so are part of the 26 weeks permitted for such leave. An employer who contravenes this requirement will be guilty of an offence and liable to a fine if convicted.[16]

An employee may also be entitled to ordinary and additional maternity leave if she satisfies certain conditions.

---

13 See Code of Practice on Employment Chapter 8 (EHRC 2011a).
14 SI 1999/3312.
15 Regulation 8 MPL Regulations.
16 Section 72(3)(b) and (5) ERA 1996.

6.5.2 Ordinary maternity leave

This can be started in a number of ways.[17] First, the employee may choose the start date, provided the notice requirements are met and provided that she does not specify a date earlier than the beginning of the eleventh week before the expected week of childbirth.[18] Second, if the employee is absent from work on any day after the beginning of the fourth week before the expected week of childbirth for a reason wholly or partly because of the pregnancy, then the ordinary leave period will automatically begin on that day. Third, if the ordinary maternity leave period has not begun by the time when the child is born, then it will begin on the day after childbirth occurs.

Ordinary maternity leave continues for a period of 26 weeks from its commencement, or until the end of the compulsory maternity leave period, whichever is later.[19] This period can be further extended if there is a statutory provision that prohibits the employee from working after the end of the ordinary maternity leave period, for a reason related to the fact that she has recently given birth. The period of leave may end early if the employee is dismissed during the period of her leave. In the event of such a dismissal, the period ends at the time of that dismissal.[20]

6.5.3 Additional maternity leave

This period commences on the day after the last day of her ordinary maternity leave period and continues for 26 weeks, meaning that all affected employees are entitled to a total of 52 weeks' leave.[21] The period of leave may end early if the employee is dismissed during the period of her leave. In the event of such a dismissal, the period ends at the time of the dismissal.[22]

So the protected period in the Equality Act 2010, which commences with notification of the pregnancy, can end after the end of ordinary or additional maternity leave, whichever is appropriate.

6.6 Employment rights

The Code of Practice on Employment (EHRC 2011a) provides a list[23] of examples of situations where to treat women less favourably might amount to pregnancy and maternity discrimination:

(i)   the fact that, because of her pregnancy, the woman will be temporarily unable to do the job for which she is specifically employed whether permanently or on a fixed-term contract;

(ii)   the pregnant woman is temporarily unable to work because to do so would be a breach of health and safety regulations;

(iii)   the costs to the business of covering her work;

(iv)   any absence due to pregnancy-related illness;

(v)   her inability to attend a disciplinary hearing due to morning sickness or other pregnancy-related conditions; and

(vi)   performance issues due to morning sickness or other pregnancy-related conditions.

The Code explains that this is not an exhaustive list.

Certain special rights are accorded to pregnant workers and those who have recently given birth or are breastfeeding, as discussed in the following sections.

---

17 Regulation 6 MPL Regulations.
18 Regulation 4(2)(b) MPL Regulations.
19 Regulation 7(1) MPL Regulations.
20 Regulation 7(5) MPL Regulations.
21 Regulation 6(3) MPL Regulations.
22 Regulation 7(4)–(5) MPL Regulations.
23 Para 8.22.

6.6.1 Time off for ante-natal care

A pregnant employee who has made an appointment to attend for ante-natal care, on the advice of a registered medical practitioner, registered midwife, or registered health visitor, is entitled to time off with pay during normal working hours to attend the appointment.[24]

6.6.2 Risk assessment and suspension from work

The Management of Health and Safety at Work (MHSW) Regulations 1999[25] requires employers to carry out a risk assessment of the risks to health and safety of employees and others. Regulation 16(1) of the MHSW Regulations 1999 requires special attention in the event of there being female employees of childbearing age. The assessment is to decide whether the work is of a kind that would pose a risk, by reason of her condition, to the health and safety of a new or expectant mother or that of her baby. The obligation to carry out this risk assessment is not confined to situations where the employer has a pregnant employee. The employment of a woman of childbearing age should be enough to set off the need for such an assessment.[26] If it is reasonable to do so, the employer can change the working hours or working conditions in order to avoid the risks.[27] If it is not reasonable to do so, then the employer must suspend the pregnant employee for as long as the risk persists. This suspension can only take place where a risk cannot be avoided.

An employee who is suspended from work as a result of a statutory prohibition, or as a result of a recommendation contained in a code of practice issued or approved under the Health and Safety at Work etc. Act 1974, is entitled to be paid during that suspension or offered alternative work.[28] The alternative work needs to be both suitable and appropriate given the employee's circumstances and the terms and conditions offered to her must not be substantially less favourable than her previous terms and conditions.

In *Pedersen*[29] it was held that national legislation that permitted the sending home of a pregnant woman in such a situation, without paying her salary in full, was contrary to the Equal Treatment Directive; legislation that only affects pregnant employees was in breach of Article 5 of the Equal Treatment Directive. Also in *British Airways (European Operations at Gatwick) Ltd v Moore and Botterill*[30] the cabin crew who could not fly during their pregnancies were employed in alternative ground-based work, but were not given the flying allowances to which they had previously been entitled when working as cabin crew. This was held to be discriminatory.

6.6.3 Maternity leave

An employee may carry out up to ten days' work for her employer during her statutory maternity period (excluding the compulsory maternity period)[31] without bringing her maternity leave period to an end.[32] This is part of a policy designed to encourage employers and those on maternity leave to keep in touch with each other and, of course, to help the return to work. Any work carried out on any day shall constitute a day's work and the work can include training or any activity designed

---

24 Sections 55–57 ERA 1996.
25 SI 1999/3242; Regulation 3(1).
26 See *Day v T Pickles Farms Ltd* [1999] IRLR 217.
27 Regulation 16(2) MHSW Regulations 1999.
28 Sections 66–68 ERA 1996.
29 Case C-66/96 *Handels og Kontorfunktionærernes Forbund i Danmark (acting for Høj Pedersen) v Fællesforeningen for Danmarks Brugsforeninger (acting for Kvickly Skive)* [1999] IRLR 55.
30 [2000] IRLR 296.
31 Regulation 12A(5) MPL Regulations.
32 Regulation 12A(1) MPL Regulations.

for the purpose of keeping in touch with the workplace.[33] Regulation 12A(6) MPL Regulations makes it clear that this does not mean that the employer has the right to require this work or that the employee has a right to work. It clearly needs to be a mutually agreed option, but one which many employers and those on maternity leave may be interested in using. The period spent working does not have the effect of extending the total duration of the maternity leave period.[34]

Section 71(4) of the ERA 1996 provides that an employee on ordinary maternity leave is, first, entitled to the benefit of the terms and conditions of employment that would have applied had she not been absent. This does not include terms and conditions about remuneration,[35] although Regulation 9 of the MPL Regulations limits the definition of remuneration to sums payable to an employee by way of wages or salary. A failure to reflect a pay increase in calculating earnings-related statutory maternity pay for an employee on maternity leave was likely to be a breach of Article 157 on equal pay and the employee would have an entitlement to make a claim for unlawful deduction from her wages.[36]

In addition, the employee is bound by obligations arising out of those terms and conditions, and she is also entitled to return from leave to the job in which she was employed before her absence. Indeed, where the contract of employment continues during pregnancy, to afford a woman less favourable treatment regarding her working conditions during that time would constitute sex discrimination within the terms of the Equal Treatment Directive.[37]

6.7 Protection from detriment

Regulation 19 of the MPL Regulations provides that an employee is not to be subjected to any detriment by any act, or failure to act, by her employer[38] for a number of specified reasons, including that the employee:

- is pregnant;
- has given birth to a child;
- took, or sought to take, the benefits of ordinary maternity leave;
- took, or sought to take, additional maternity leave; or
- failed to return after a period of ordinary or additional maternity leave and undertook, considered undertaking or refused to undertake work that is allowed during the maternity leave period.

Examples of actions by employers that have been held to be discriminatory are, first, when an employer[39] held a disciplinary hearing without the attendance of the pregnant employee, who was absent on a pregnancy-related illness. The employee had given notice of the date when she wished her maternity leave to begin whilst she was absent through pregnancy-related sickness. The employers wished to resolve the matter prior to the maternity leave and proceeded with the hearing, even though the employee's doctor considered that she was unfit to attend the meeting and would be so until the end of her pregnancy. Second, in *Green and McLaughlin*,[40] when two

---

33 Regulation 12A(2) and (3) MPL Regulations.
34 Regulation 12A(7) MPL Regulations.
35 Section 71(5) ERA 1996.
36 See *Alabaster v Woolwich plc and Secretary of State for Social Security* [2000] IRLR 754.
37 Case C-136/95 *Caisse National d'Assurance Vieillesse des Travailleurs Salariés v Thibault* [1998] IRLR 399, where a woman on maternity leave was not given an annual appraisal and was, as a result, deprived of a merit pay award.
38 See section 47C ERA 1996.
39 *Abbey National plc v Formoso* [1999] IRLR 222.
40 *Gus Home Shopping Ltd v Green and McLaughlin* [2001] IRLR 75.

employees who were absent from work because of their pregnancy did not receive a discretionary loyalty bonus payable to all employees who remained in their posts until a business transferred to a new location. The different treatment meant that they had been unlawfully discriminated against on the grounds of sex.

6.8 Protection from detriment and dismissal

If, during an employee's absence by reason of pregnancy, her job becomes redundant, the employee is entitled to be offered any suitable alternative vacancy before the end of her employment under a new contract of employment, which takes effect immediately upon ending employment under the current contract. This applies to vacancies with the employer, their successor or an associated employer. The new contract of employment must be such that the work to be done is of a kind that is both suitable in relation to the employee and appropriate for her to do in the circumstances, and the terms and conditions of employment and the capacity and location in which she is to be employed are not substantially less favourable than had she continued to be employed under her previous contract of employment.[41] If the employee is not offered available alternative employment, then she may be regarded as being unfairly dismissed.

The MPL Regulations[42] also provide that if an employee is dismissed for reasons of redundancy and it is shown that the circumstances constituting the redundancy applied equally to one or more other employees in the same undertaking who held similar positions to the dismissed employee, and those other employees have not been dismissed, and the reason, or the principal reason, for the employee being selected for dismissal was related to her pregnancy (as in protection from detriment above), then the dismissal will be also be unfair.

There are a number of relevant reasons for dismissal that will be regarded as unfair. If the reason, or the principal reason, for the dismissal is:

1. the pregnancy of the employee or the fact that she has given birth to a child, during her ordinary or additional maternity leave period; or
2. the application of a relevant requirement, or a relevant recommendation in accordance with the provisions concerning suspension from work on maternity grounds; or
3. the fact that she undertook, considered undertaking or refused to undertake work in accordance with Regulation 12A;[43] or
4. the fact that she took or availed herself of the benefits of ordinary and additional maternity leave;

then the dismissal is unfair.[44]

The difficulties that this strict policy can cause is shown in *Cromwell Garage v Doran*.[45] The respondent was a small garage with a shop. Mrs Doran, who had three children, worked as forecourt manager and also covered the shop. She told her boss, Mr Lynch, that she was pregnant and 'he made a number of comments', including that she was 'dropping him in it' and about the inability of women to run a family and a job. Before her return date, Mrs Doran had three meetings with Mr Lynch. He tried to persuade her to change her hours of work to suit the business. She refused and was eventually dismissed. The Respondent, who lost, complained that the Tribunal

---

41 Regulation 10(2)–(3) MPL Regulations.
42 Regulation 20(2).
43 Regulation 19 MPL Regulations.
44 Regulation 20 MPL Regulations.
45 UKEAT/0369/10/ZT.

failed to pay sufficient attention to the problems of a small business. It is a difficult situation, but it was clear that discrimination had taken place.

In *Eversheds Legal Services Ltd v De Belin*[46] the employer was faced with a choice between dismissing a male employee or a woman on maternity leave for reasons of redundancy. The employer awarded notional points to the employee on maternity leave, which enabled her to score more points with the result that the male employee was made redundant. He brought and succeeded in a claim for sex discrimination. The EAT held that the means used to compensate for the disadvantage of being absent on maternity leave were not proportionate. The court stated that the words 'special treatment afforded to women in connection with pregnancy or childbirth' referred only to treatment given to a woman:

> so far as it constitutes a proportionate means of achieving the legitimate aim of compensating her for the disadvantages occasioned by her pregnancy or her maternity leave.

It was pointed out during the case that the employer was in a difficult position and likely to face a complaint no matter what decision was taken. If the employer had made the woman on maternity leave redundant, then it may have faced a claim form her.

6.9 Return to work

An employee who wishes to return early from her additional maternity leave period must give her employer at least eight weeks' notice of the date on which she intends to return. If the employee tries to return early without giving this notice, then the employer may delay her return for eight weeks.[47]

An employee's right to return from leave to the job in which she was employed before her absence[48] means that she has a right to return both with her seniority, pension and other similar rights intact as if she had not been absent, and with terms and conditions no less favourable than those that would have applied had she not been absent.[49] Except where there is a genuine redundancy situation leading to the dismissal, an employee who takes ordinary or additional maternity leave is entitled to return to the job in which she was employed before her absence.[50] If it is not reasonably practicable for an employer to permit her to do so, then she may return to another job that is both suitable and appropriate for her in the circumstances. This right is to return on terms and conditions no less favourable than would have been applicable had she not been absent from work at any time since the beginning of the ordinary maternity leave period. This includes returning with her seniority, pension rights and similar rights as if she had been in continuous employment during the periods of leave and not any less favourable than if she had not been absent through taking additional maternity leave after the ordinary maternity leave period.[51]

6.10 Summary

In this chapter we have considered the special protection given to women during pregnancy and maternity leave (the protected period). Although pregnancy and maternity is now a protected

---

46 [2011] IRLR 448.
47 Regulation 11 MPL Regulations.
48 Section 71(4)(c) ERA 1996.
49 Section 71(7) ERA 1996.
50 Regulation 18(2) MPL Regulations.
51 Regulation 18(5) MPL Regulations.

characteristic contained in the Equality Act 2010, much of the protection comes from other pieces of legislation and such protection has a long history in the courts, especially at the Court of Justice. Despite pregnancy and maternity being a protected characteristic, any detriment caused will likely amount to sex discrimination. As the *Eversheds* case shows, this protection needs to be proportionate in relation to other employees. Despite this, the protection offered is fairly uncompromising and women in this position receive strong protection. It perhaps shows the limits of the law, however, when one realises that, despite this, many thousands of women lose their jobs every year because they become pregnant.

Chapter 7

Race, Colour, Ethnicity and Migrant Workers

7.1 Introduction

The United Kingdom is an ethnically diverse country and is becoming more so. In England and Wales, for example, the non-white British population grew by an average of 4.1% each year from 2001 to 2009. This compared to an almost static white British group during this period. The biggest percentage increase during this period was the Chinese ethnic group, although the Asian–Indian group remains the biggest non-white group numerically, followed by the Asian–Pakistani group. The outcome is that some one in six people living in England and Wales are from a non-white background. This diversity is seen at its best in London where, by 2031, 39% of London's population is projected to be from a BAME[1] group. This compares with 32% in 2006 and 29% in 2001. As a comparison, in 1991 all ethnic groups other than white were estimated to form 20% of London's population. By 2025, seven London boroughs are projected to have BAME populations that represent over 50% of the total.[2] The importance of this growing diversity is shown by the fact that, between 2006 and 2031, London's population of economically active ages is projected to grow by 840,000, an increase of 16%. Sixty-nine per cent of the growth will be attributable to the BAME population.[3]

In 2004, when a number of countries joined the EU, Member States were given the option, for a limited period, to stop workers from eight of the new States coming to their countries to work, for a period of up to seven years. The United Kingdom did not do this, but instead introduced a workers registration scheme (WRS) for these new workers. The scale of the resulting migration was considerably larger than the government estimated at the time. The total number of approved applicants[4] under the WRS between May 2004 and June 2008 was 853,850. The highest proportion of approved applications were from Polish nationals (67%), followed by those from Slovakia (10%) and Lithuania (9%). These figures do not reflect the total inflow of migrant workers and it is likely that the actual total figure was much higher, taking into account illegal migration, self-employed migrants and migrants from other countries such as Bulgaria and Romania. These numbers fell significantly from 2008 onwards as a result of difficult economic conditions, which resulted in large job losses in areas of the economy in which many of the A8 workers were employed.[5] The outcome is that there is now also a significant white population from outside the UK.

Despite almost fifty years of legislation against race discrimination, it still exists everywhere. The first Race Relations Act was enacted in 1965, but did not include employment or the concept of indirect discrimination. There was a further Race Relations Act in 1968, which was eventually followed by the 1976 Race Relations Act, which did distinguish between direct and indirect discrimination. This has now been replaced by the Equality Act 2010. The continuation of discrimination against race is evidenced by the fact that unemployment rates for the non-white population are significantly higher than for the white population. At the end of 2011, for example, the unemployment rate for young white people (aged 16–24 years) was a distressing 20.8%, but for young Asians it was 26.7% and for young black people in the same age range it was an appalling 47.4%. Racist incidents reported to the police are in decline but still remain high. In 2008/9 there were 55,714 such reports made to the police, in 2009/10 this figure was 54,872 and in 2010/11 the figure was 51,187 (Home Office 2011). These figures are for England and Wales and it is not unreasonable to assume that, in addition, there are many racist incidents that do not get reported to the police.

---

1 BAME – Black, Asian and Minority Ethnic.
2 Harrow, Redbridge, Ealing, Hounslow, Croydon, Brent and Newham.
3 GLA Intelligence Update 2010, available at: http://www.london.gov.uk/sites/default/files/DMAG%20Update%2004-2010% 20R2008%20London%20Plan%20Ethnic%20Group%20Population%20Projections.pdf (last accessed 17 January 2013).
4 The eight States that joined the EU in 2004 and whose citizens benefitted from the ability to move freely to the UK for work after this date are the Czech Republic, Estonia, Hungary, Latvia, Lithuania, Poland, Slovakia and Slovenia (also referred to as the A8).
5 See, for example, the estimates contained in Capital Economics London 2007.

7.2 The Race Directive

The EU has a long and positive record on the subject of sex discrimination and equal pay, but has a lesser record on the subject of race discrimination. The first Directive aimed at tackling such discrimination was adopted in 2000.[6] Article 1 of the Directive provides that:

> The purpose of this Directive is to lay down a framework for combating discrimination on the grounds of racial or ethnic origin, with a view to putting into effect in the Member States the principle of equal treatment.

According to Article 2(1), the principle of equal treatment means that there should be no direct or indirect discrimination on the grounds of racial or ethnic origin. Article 3 also prohibits harassment related to ethnic or racial origin. A good example of the Court of Justice's positive approach to interpreting the Directive can be seen in the case of *Firma Feryn*.[7] In this case a Belgian employer, which specialised in the sale and installation of 'up and over' doors, was looking to recruit new fitters. One of the directors of the company made public statements to the effect that it could not employ 'immigrants' because its customers were reluctant to give them access to their private residences for the duration of the work. The Court of Justice clearly stated that:

> The fact that an employer declares publicly that it will not recruit employees of a certain ethnic or racial origin, something which is clearly likely to strongly dissuade certain candidates from submitting their candidature and, accordingly, to hinder their access to the labour market, constitutes direct discrimination in respect of recruitment within the meaning of Directive 2000/43.

There are, as with the other protected characteristics, two exceptions to this general prohibition of discrimination contained in the Directive. One is for a 'genuine and determining occupational requirement' so that an exception can be made 'by reason of the nature of the particular occupational activities concerned or of the context in which they are carried out'.[8] The second exception is contained in Article 5 and provides the opportunity for positive action measures. This is considered in Chapter 1, but here it is worth remembering the difference between positive action and positive discrimination. Generally speaking, the first is permissible, but the second is not. Since the early 1960s the American approach has been to introduce a policy of affirmative action. It results from a belief that achieving equality requires something more than just making discrimination unlawful. It requires something much more positive and can amount to positive discrimination in favour of under-represented groups such as those from black or ethnic minorities. Positive discrimination in favour of such groups might be interpreted as amounting to discrimination against white people and that, of course, is the problem. In the USA it had its roots in the civil rights movement of the 1960s and the desire to end segregation in the educational system by reserving places for people from minorities.

7.3 The Equality Act 2010

Section 4 of the Equality Act 2010 provides that race is one of the nine protected characteristics. As with the other protected characteristics, the Equality Act makes direct discrimination, indirect

---

6 Council Directive 2000/43/EC implementing the principle of equal treatment between persons irrespective of racial or ethnic origin.
7 Case C-54/07 *Centrum Voor Gelijkheid Van Kansen En Voor Racismebestrijding v Firma Freyn NV* [2008] IRLR 732.
8 Article 4.

discrimination, harassment and victimisation on the characteristic of race unlawful. Section 9(1) provides that the term race includes colour, nationality and ethnic or national origins. A reference to a person sharing one of these characteristics with others is a reference to a racial group.[9] Interestingly there is also provision for a further protected characteristic to be added, namely that of caste.[10]

7.3.1 Caste

According to government research published in 2010 (Government Equalities Office 2010), the term 'caste' is used to identify a number of different concepts, notably, *varna* (a Hindu religious caste system), *jati* (an occupational caste system) and *biraderi* (often referred to as a clan system). The types of discrimination described in the report of the research included workplace bullying, the provision of services and pupil on pupil bullying in education. The discrimination was always by 'higher' castes to 'lower' ones. The report concluded with this statement:

> The study found evidence of caste discrimination and harassment in Britain in areas relevant to the Equality Act 2010, namely in work and the provision of services. It also found evidence of caste discrimination and harassment in other areas, namely education (pupil against pupil bullying), voluntary work (dismissal), worship and religion and public behaviour (harassment in public places). The consequences of these could be severe for the victims.

Clearly there can be an overlap between race discrimination and caste discrimination, but the government has yet to decide whether to implement section 9(5) of the Equality Act and make caste a tenth protected characteristic.

7.3.2 Colour

Here are two cases that illustrate the wide scope and the limitations of the protection offered. The first is about a white employee instructed to take discriminatory decisions based on apparent race; the second concerns the problem of employing a white person with extreme views alongside many people having the colour or ethnic origin that his political party would be unlikely to admit.

It is possible for a person to be unfavourably treated on racial grounds even if the claimant is not a member of the group being discriminated against. In *Weathersfield v Sargent*[11] a person of white European ancestry obtained a job as a receptionist for a van and truck rental company. During her induction course she was given instructions on how to assess different classes of people for risk. She was told that the company had a special policy towards potential customers from ethnic minorities, and was instructed that:

> if you get a telephone call from any coloured or Asians you can usually tell them by the sound of their voice. You have to tell them that there are no vehicles available.

Mrs Sargent, to her credit, was so upset by this policy that she decided that she could not continue in the job and resigned, claiming constructive dismissal on the grounds that she had been unfavourably treated on racial grounds. The Court of Appeal held that it was appropriate to give a broad meaning to the expression 'racial grounds'. In this case it included an employee who was required to carry out a racially discriminatory policy, even though the instruction concerned

---

9 Sections 9(2) and 9(3) Equality Act 2010.
10 Section 9(5) Equality Act 2010.
11 [1999] IRLR 94.

others of a different racial group. It was an expression that should be capable of covering any reason or action based on race.

In *Redfearn v SERCO Ltd*[12] a white man was employed as a bus driver and as an escort for children and adults with special needs. A newspaper article identified him as a candidate for the British National Party at the local elections for Bradford City Council. Membership of this party was restricted to white people only. He was successfully elected to the Council. The trade union, UNISON, wrote to the Council saying that Mr Redfearn's presence was a matter of concern, given this 'overt and racist agenda'. Some 70–80 per cent of the bus company's passengers were of Asian origin, as were some 35 per cent of the employer's workforce. He was dismissed on health and safety grounds because of the feared reaction of other employees and passengers. Although it was not claimed that he brought his political views into the workplace, there was a fear of violence and/ or anger by other employees as well as a concern about the reaction of Asian passengers with whom Mr Redfearn might travel. He did not have enough service to bring a claim for unfair dismissal, but he did claim both direct and indirect race discrimination. He lost his claim at the Employment Tribunal but was successful on appeal to the EAT. According to the EAT, the Employment Tribunal had failed to consider whether the health and safety grounds were themselves influenced by considerations of race.

The Court of Appeal, however, supported the view that he had been dismissed on racial grounds, although it did state that discrimination on racial grounds is not restricted to less favourable treatment on the grounds of the colour of the applicant. White persons could be treated less favourably than other white persons on the grounds of colour, for example in the case of a white person being dismissed after marrying a black person or a white publican refusing to admit or serve a white customer on the grounds that he is accompanied by a black person.

7.3.3 Nationality and national origins

According to the Code of Practice on Employment (EHRC 2011a), the term nationality describes the legal relationship between a person and a State, resulting from birth or naturalisation.[13] Nationality is to be distinguished from national origins. National origins, according to the Code of Practice, 'must have identifiable elements, both historic and geographic, which at least at some point in time indicate the existence or previous existence of a nation'.[14] So the English and Scots have separate national origins because England and Scotland were once separate nations. An example of the difference might be those who have a Chinese national origin and may be citizens of China, but they may also be citizens of another country.[15]

7.3.4 Ethnicity

The definition of what constitutes an ethnic group was established in the case of *Mandla v Dowell Lee*.[16] This case resulted from a school refusing to change its school uniform policy to allow the wearing of turbans. This stopped a boy's application to join the school, because his father wished him to be brought up as a practising Sikh, which required the wearing of a turban. The boy's father complained to the Commission for Racial Equality (now the Equality and Human Rights Commission), which took up the case. In order to establish that racial discrimination had taken place in terms of the Equality Act, it was necessary for Sikhs to be defined as a racial group. The argument centred on

---

12 [2006] IRLR 623.
13 Para 2.38.
14 Para 2.43.
15 Paras 2.43 and 2.44.
16 [1983] IRLR 209.

whether they were an ethnic group. The House of Lords decided that there were a number of conditions to be met before a group could call itself an ethnic group. Lord Fraser stated:

> The conditions which appear to me to be essential are these: – (1) a long, shared history, of which the group is conscious as distinguishing it from other groups, and the memory of which it keeps alive; (2) a cultural tradition of its own, including family and social customs and manners, often but not necessarily associated with religious observance. In addition to those two essential characteristics the following characteristics are, in my opinion, relevant: (3) either a common geographical origin, or a descent from a small number of common ancestors; (4) a common language, not necessarily peculiar to the group; (5) a common literature peculiar to the group; (6) a common religion different from that of neighbouring groups or from the general community surrounding it; (7) being a minority or being an oppressed or a dominant group within a larger community.

Such a group could include converts to it or persons who have married into it. Thus the term 'ethnic' could have a wide meaning.

This definition is adopted by the Code of Practice on Employment, which stated[17] that the two essential elements in defining an ethnic group are a long-shared history and the group having a cultural tradition of its own. In addition the group may share one or all of having a common language; a common literature; a common religion; a common geographical origin; or being a minority or an oppressed group.

This definition did not extend to Rastafarians, however. In *Dawkins*[18] an applicant for a job was turned away because he was a Rastafarian and would not comply with a requirement for short hair. His complaint of discrimination was rejected by the Court of Appeal on the grounds that Rastafarians could not be defined as a racial group under the Race Relations Act 1976. They did not fulfil the criteria laid down in *Mandla v Dowell Lee* because they did not have a long-shared history,[19] and could not be compared as a racial group to the Jamaican community or the Afro-Caribbean community in England.

R v *Governing Body of JFS*[20] concerned an application for admission to the Jewish Free School. It was described as a school that was Orthodox Jewish in character. The school had a policy of giving preference to those whose status as Jews was recognised by the Chief Rabbi's office. An important aspect of this is that the child of a Jewish mother is automatically Jewish. The problem for the applicant was that his father was born Jewish, but his mother was a convert to Judaism, although not until after his birth. Conversion to Orthodox Judaism was a long and difficult process, but conversion to other denominations of Judaism was a shorter process and this was the route followed by the applicant's mother. The Supreme Court distinguished between using the Orthodox criteria and the *Mandla* criteria. It stated that:

> The cohort identified by the *Mandla* criteria forms the Jewish ethnic group. They no longer have a common geographical origin or descent from a small number of common ancestors, but they share what Lord Fraser regarded as the essentials, a long shared history, of which the group is conscious as distinguishing it from other groups and the memory of which it keeps alive and a cultural tradition of its own, including family and social customs and manners, often but not necessarily associated with religious observance. The man in the street would recognise a

---

17 Para 2.40.
18 *Dawkins v Department of the Environment; sub nom Crown Suppliers PSA* [1993] IRLR 284 CA.
19 Only 60 years was suggested by the court.
20 R v *Governing Body of JFS and the Admissions Appeal Panel of JFS* [2010] IRLR 136.

member of this group as a Jew, and discrimination on the ground of membership of the group as racial discrimination.

The applicant was refused admission to the school on the basis that his mother's conversion was not in accordance with Orthodox standards. The court upheld his complaint of racial discrimination. The conversion of the mother had, using the *Mandla* definition, brought her within the Jewish ethnic group and it followed that the applicant had been refused admission because of his membership of the ethnic group. It was irrelevant that this was done to comply with religious law rather than a concern with the ethnicity of the candidate.

7.3.5 Segregation

Section 13(5) Equality Act provides that:

> If the protected characteristic is race, less favourable treatment includes segregating B from others.

Thus, when the protected characteristic is race, deliberately segregating a worker or group of workers from others of a different race automatically amounts to less favourable treatment. There is no need to identify a comparator, because racial segregation is always discriminatory.[21] The Code of Practice provides the following example:

> A British marketing company which employs predominantly British staff recruits Polish nationals and seats them in a separate room nicknamed 'Little Poland'. The company argues that they have an unofficial policy of seating the Polish staff separately from British staff so that they can speak amongst themselves in their native language without disturbing the staff who speak English. This is segregation, as the company has a deliberate policy of separating staff because of race.

7.4 Migrant workers

Migration is an important issue when considering the subject of race discrimination. Despite the contribution that they make to their host countries, migrants often face serious labour market disadvantages.[22] In *Counting the Cost: Working Conditions of Migrants* (EIRO 2008) issues relating to detriment in employment are considered. In job-seeking, for instance, a French survey found that men with French or European-sounding names were five times more likely to be called for interview than applicants with equivalent qualifications and experience but with North African names. Overall, according to this study, migrants face a greater likelihood of unemployment than nationals, certain groups being especially disadvantaged – non-EU nationals, younger people, and women. In many countries migrant workers are more likely to work on fixed-term contracts, and less likely to be retained in employment. Some countries have a policy of issuing short-term work permits: hence, workers can only take jobs of limited duration. Many migrants work in seasonal sectors, and in some countries temporary employment agencies are a key recruiter of migrant workers. While such non-standard jobs could potentially lead to stable employment, a Swedish study suggested that fixed-term contracts lead to stable jobs for migrant workers less often than for Swedish workers. The

---

21 Para 3.8 Code of Practice on Employment.
22 See, for example, Spencer 2008.

study further comments that migrant workers tend to be segregated into low-skilled jobs in such sectors as services, construction and manufacturing, given the language and legal barriers that hinder them from accessing skilled occupations. Hence, as a group they have less job security, run the risk of more accidents at work and are generally more likely to employed in unhealthy occupations. Working in such sectors also means that they are likely to be paid less; in Italy, for example, non-EU workers earn around half of the national average wage.

Having a higher level of education boosts an individual's opportunities for employment. However, according to this study, Organisation for Economic Co-operation and Development (OECD) statistics for 2006 indicate that skilled migrants had lower rates of employment than skilled nationals. An example is given of the situation in Germany where German nationals with a third-level qualification had an employment rate of 84.5 per cent, as against 68.1 per cent for non-nationals. For those with a lower level of education, the differences were not as marked and unskilled migrants may even have higher employment rates than their native counterparts. In the same year lower-skilled German nationals had an employment rate of 40.2 per cent, whereas for their non-national counterparts it was 45.1 per cent. This indicates that migrants gain a lower return on their educational investment than do nationals, because they are more likely to find themselves in unskilled jobs.

A study of migrant women in the EU labour force (Rubin et al. 2008) divided the EU into four groupings. First, in the 'old' migrant-receiving countries (Belgium, France, Netherlands, United Kingdom and Austria) the labour force participation rates of third-country migrant women are substantially lower than those of native-born women. Second, in the 'new' migrant-receiving countries of Southern Europe (Greece, Spain, Portugal) the labour force participation rates of third-country migrant women are higher than those of native-born women. Third, the 'Nordic' countries of Denmark and Sweden vary in how recent have been their migrant flows, but are more closely associated with the old migrant-receiving countries. Finally, in the 2004 accession countries there is a much more heterogeneous pattern of participation. Most migrant women in the new receiving countries are younger and this may explain the higher levels of participation. Two major determinants of migrant women's participation rates are the age of the youngest child and how recently the migrant arrived in the receiving country. Unemployment rates of third-country migrant women are higher than those of third-country migrant men.

The study also found that temporary contract employment is a further source of disadvantage for migrant women. The highest proportion of temporary employment contracts amongst employed migrant women are found in the 'new' migrant-receiving countries of Southern Europe (also in Cyprus and the Czech Republic). In both Spain and Cyprus more than half of employed migrant women have temporary employment contracts. In the 'old' migrant-receiving countries only Sweden has a high proportion of such contracts. The analysis states that:

> This results in a 'double disadvantage' conclusion for migrant women in the 'new' migrant-receiving countries: 'unemployment and underemployment' is more prevalent among migrant women than among native-born women, and is more prevalent still than among migrant men.

The analysis found that migrant women are concentrated in a small number of sectors for employment purposes – 62 per cent of them work in five sectors: sales and service elementary occupations; personal and protective services; office clerks; other associate professionals; and models, salespersons and demonstrators. There is a concentration in the lowest skills sectors.

The International Labour Organization report titled 'Towards a fair deal for migrant workers in the global economy' (ILO 2004) suggests that there are two aspects of health issues for migrant workers. The first is related to occupational health and safety (OHS) at the workplace; and the second concerns the general health condition of the migrant worker and her family. Health is an important issue because, as the report states, first, migrant workers tend to be employed in high-risk occupations; second, that there are language and cultural barriers to OHS communication, in particular OHS training and instruction; and, third, many of the migrant workers overwork and/or suffer from poor general health, and so are susceptible to occupational injuries and work-related diseases. The Report also states that:

> Occupational accident rates are about twice as high for migrant workers as for native workers in Europe, and there is no reason to believe that the situation is any different in other parts of the world.

In terms of seeking assistance, temporary workers, and in particular migrants in an irregular status, are often not able to access social security benefits such as those relating to employment injuries and occupational illnesses. They often do not seek medical treatment because 'of the cost, inability to take time off work, lack of childcare, and problems of transportation. Many are unfamiliar with the local health-care systems and may have linguistic or cultural difficulties in communicating their problems'.

Domestic workers are especially vulnerable to discrimination, exploitation and abuse, without this necessarily being trafficking or forced labour. There are a number of issues to be dealt with. First, when many domestic workers lose their employment, they sometimes also lose resident status. Examples of tackling this are Canada, where a 'bridge extension' has been introduced, whereby a two-month interim work permit may be issued during the period when the worker is looking for another job; and Israel where a worker may obtain a 30-day tourist visa to cover this period. Second, providing safe houses as temporary accommodation, accompanied by an efficient support network, is crucial. Some countries have done this in States where their nationals are employed as domestic workers. Third, work permits should not have a condition that requires the worker to live in the employer's home. This can be an encouragement to forced labour. Finally, abuse by some employment agencies need to be controlled.

The Report suggests that there are examples of best practice to improve working conditions for migrant workers. These include:

- having competent institutions to supervise recruitment and migration;
- encouraging migrants to sign contracts that have been approved by competent national authorities;
- including migrant workers in work-related health programmes;
- use of bridging arrangements; and
- establishing agencies to monitor and to seek to reduce discrimination.

The Report applies this to migrant women domestic workers who, it claims, are amongst the world's most vulnerable workers.

7.5 Precarious work

An OSHA[23] 'expert forecast' in 2007 on emerging psychosocial risks related to occupational safety and health stated that there was growing evidence that there are specific risks for health and safety in the workplace connected with the conditions that characterise these forms of work. Their report cited Rodgers and Rodgers (1989) as proposing four dimensions to precarious working:

---

23 Occupational Health and Safety Administration in the USA.

- the low level of certainty over the continuity of employment;
- low individual and collective control over work (working conditions, income, working hours);
- low level of protection (social protection, protection against unemployment, or against discrimination); and
- insufficient income or economic vulnerability.

Precariousness, according to the report, is caused by a combination of these elements rather than by one aspect only. Work bearing such characteristics is generally considered to increase the risk of illness and injury. Precarious work takes different forms in today's job market. In the scientific literature it is often associated with non-standard forms of work such as temporary, part-time, on-call, day-hire or short-term positions and also with the increase in the prevalence of self-employment. Additionally, work at home and multiple jobs also contribute to the increasing significance of 'non-standard' forms when considering precarious work. The employees who seem to be at a special risk of precarious employment are migrant workers.

7.6 The TUC Commission

The Trades Union Congress in the UK set up a Commission on Vulnerable Employment, as a result of concern that unsafe, low-paid, insecure work is causing misery for millions of workers in the UK. It took the view that the well-being of any single employee and that employee's family is too important to be left unprotected. The TUC's final report is entitled *Hard Work Hidden Lives* (TUC 2008). The TUC devoted the first chapter of the report to providing its own definition of vulnerable working. The report first defines vulnerable employment as 'precarious work that places people at risk of continuous poverty and injustices resulting in an imbalance of power in the employer–worker relationship'. The report finds (p 13) that:

> Vulnerable work is insecure and low paid, placing workers at high risk of employment rights abuse. It offers very little chance of progression and few opportunities of collective action to improve conditions. Those already facing the greatest disadvantage are more likely to be in such jobs and less likely to be able to move out of them. Vulnerable employment also places workers at greater risk of experiencing problems and mistreatment at work, though fear of dismissal by those in low-paid sectors with high levels of temporary work means they are often unable to challenge it.

The Commissioners believe that much exploitation of workers occurs because the law is not strong enough to prevent it. Some employers find gaps in the law, but others break the law. It found that in certain low-paid sectors, including care, cleaning, hospitality, security and construction, there was evidence that the law was regularly broken. It believed that enforcement agencies did not have enough resources to guarantee employment rights.

The government established a 'Vulnerable Worker Enforcement Forum' in June 2007. It brought together trade unions, workplace enforcement agencies, business groups and advice bodies to look at evidence about the nature and extent of abuse of workplace rights. It published its final report in 2008.[24] In Chapter 2 it highlighted the employment rights abuses suffered by vulnerable workers:

---

24 Vulnerable Worker Enforcement Forum 2008.

Breaches of employment rights highlighted

- No written terms of engagement.
- Workers being paid below the minimum wage and not being paid for all the hours worked.
- Unauthorised deductions being made from wages.
- Holiday pay not being paid.
- Wages and holiday pay owed not being provided after leaving a job.
- Inadequate rest breaks being given.
- Excessive hours.
- Workers not being provided with safety equipment.
- The provision of sub-standard 'tied' accommodation.

There was an interesting analysis of calls made to a national helpline (run by the Advisory, Conciliation and Arbitration Service – ACAS) and the questions from those who used the language translation facility available (see Table 7.1).

Those using the non-English speaking helpline were much more concerned with issues related to holidays and working time, wages and the national minimum wage (NMW) than the overall average.

Another important issue was the awareness of vulnerable workers of their employment rights. The percentage of workers who reported not being very well informed, or not informed at all, about employment rights are shown in Table 7.2.[25]

Other issues identified were:

- A reluctance amongst vulnerable workers to report problems.
- Confusion about where to complain.
- Poor language skills for some migrant workers.
- Overseas domestic workers vulnerable to abuse
- Use of the informal economy.

In respect of the informal economy, the report stated that 'workers employed in the informal economy are at a high risk of not receiving basic rights such as the national minimum wage, paid

Table 7.1 Analysis of calls made by workers to the ACAS helpline using the Language Line service

Subject matter of call	% of language line calls	All worker calls %
Holidays and working time	29	12
Wages and NMW	26	8
Discipline, dismissal and grievance	17	23
Contracts	9	17
Maternity, paternity and adoption	8	8
Diversity and discrimination	5	4
Absence, sickness and stress	3	5
Redundancies, lay offs, business transfers	1	15
Family friendly policies	0	3
Others	2	5

25 Taken from 'Employment Rights at Work – Survey of Employees 2005', BERR.

Table 7.2 Vulnerable workers' knowledge of their employment rights

All workers	34%
Young workers	48%
Low-paid earning under £15,000	44%
Part-time workers	40%
Workers in small workplaces (1–9 employees)	40%

holiday and statutory sick pay; and the existence of an informal economy also undercuts reputable businesses. Unions represented on the Forum also pointed to bogus self-employment as being a problem, particularly in the construction sector. Workers in this position do not usually receive basic employment rights.

A report by the Citizens Advice Bureau (2007), *Rooting Out the Rogues*, while highlighting the problem of bad employers in general terms, emphasises the vulnerability of migrant workers:

> Whilst the vast majority of employers try hard to meet their legal obligations to their workforce, there are still far too many unscrupulous or rogue employers (and employment agencies) prepared to flout the law and so profit from exploitation. As a result, many tens of thousands of the most vulnerable workers from the newly expanded European Union and elsewhere are failing to benefit from the Government's very welcome policy programme since 1997 to establish a framework of decent standards in the workplace.

7.7 Health and safety

A report for the HSE (McKay et al. 2006) looked at the health and safety risks associated with migrant workers in the UK. It revealed that migrant workers were at a greater health and safety risk than others because of:

- relatively short periods of work in the UK;
- limited knowledge of the UK's health and safety system;
- different experiences of health and safety regimes in countries of origin;
- motivations in coming to the UK, particularly where these are premised on earning as much as possible, in the shortest possible time;
- ability to communicate effectively with other workers and with supervisors, particularly in relation to their understanding of risk;
- access to limited health and safety training and their difficulties in understanding what is being offered, where proficiency in English is limited;
- failure of employers to check on their skills for work and on their language skills;
- employment relationships and unclear responsibilities for health and safety, in particular where workers are supplied by recruitment agencies or labour providers or are self-employed; and
- lack of knowledge of health and safety rights and how to raise them, including knowledge of the channels through which they can be represented.

The main issues raised in the report, which was based upon a qualitative analysis of some 200 migrant workers are set out below in extracts taken directly from the report.

    (a)   Demographics of the migrant group

            Practically all the migrants interviewed were working with other migrant workers. In some cases, a particular nationality might be dominant but in others, the workforce could consist of workers from many different countries, speaking different languages and with different skills and experiences and knowledge of health and safety systems.

(b)   Access to work and recruitment

The most likely method of accessing work was through word of mouth. Employers indicated that whereas they initially may have used recruitment agencies or labour providers to supply migrant workers, as their number in the workplace increased supply through agencies was being replaced by word of mouth recruitment directly to the workplace.

(c)   Use of recruitment agencies or labour providers

Although some workers were grateful for the assistance they had received from recruitment agencies or labour providers in obtaining work, the majority of those surveyed had negative experiences of working through agencies. They reported being paid less, having unexplained deductions from wages, having irregular work and not being clear where responsibility for their health and safety lay.

(d)   Working hours and holidays

Although in the Cleaning sector some migrants were working only a few hours a day, the pattern of migrant work was that working hours are long. There were a variety of reasons for this. First, in some of the sectors in which they were employed, for example Agriculture, long working hours are routine. Second, migrant workers were more willing to work long hours because in this way they could increase their earnings and their primary aim in coming to the UK was after all to earn money.

(e)   Health and safety training

More than a third of the migrants interviewed had not received any training in health and safety and for the remaining two-thirds the training that had been offered was generally limited to a short session at induction. But there were some differences by sector, for example those in Public Healthcare had longer periods of induction training and were more likely to be offered ongoing training.

Communicating health and safety training where there is no common language presents challenges to employers and some had responded by developing means of conveying information through non-verbal mediums. Migrant workers particularly welcomed visual aids, as they could overcome the limitations that a lack of English presented. However, the greater the range of methods used to communicate, the more successful they were perceived to be by the workers interviewed. Any single method used exclusively was unlikely to deliver a comprehensive message, understood by all workers.

(f)   The system of health and safety in the workplace

There was a widespread lack of knowledge of basic health and safety procedures, including fire safety. Although most workers had been provided with some protective clothing, this often failed to take account of the fact that workers had difficulty in acclimatising themselves to the different environmental conditions they experienced in the UK, in contrast to their own country. In addition, since many migrant workers had not previously worked in the occupations they were following in the UK, acclimatisation was sometimes a difficulty, particularly where migrants did not possess suitable clothing even though they were working outside or inside but in chill departments. Allocation to the least desirable work also meant that workers were more likely to be working in areas that experienced extremes of temperature. Workers consequently fell ill more frequently and in general believed that their health had suffered as a consequence of the work they were doing.

(g)   Appropriate health and safety for a transient workforce

The investigation of health and safety incidents is made more difficult where there is little incentive for the migrant worker to remain in the UK and that is more likely to be the case where the incident would require time off work. Since the primary purpose of migration is to earn money, remaining in the UK without being able to work appears to serve no useful purpose to the migrant worker who is generally faced with higher living costs in this country. The migrant workers interviewed rarely had access to occupational sick pay or knowledge of its existence.

(h) Undocumented and unauthorised workers

Among those interviewees who were undocumented the fact that they were working without documentation meant that they were at greater risk of dismissal where the employer feared an immigration raid. The effect could drive undocumented workers further into forms of work that presented greater risks to their health and safety.

(i) Discrimination and racism

One of the issues migrant workers raised in the course of the interviews was their experience of discriminatory treatment at work, often related to their nationality or status. Many of the workers interviewed believed that they and migrant workers generally were often allocated to the worst shifts, were denied concessions that were available to local workers and had less favourable terms and conditions.

(j) Knowledge of English within the migrant group

Only half of those interviewed had good or perfect English and many workers asserted that their inability to speak English was the reason why they were working below their qualifications or skills. Workers admitted to pretending to understand English for fear of not getting work or losing their jobs if their lack of English was known. But this had implications, particularly in relation to health and safety training, where some of those interviewed admitted that they had not been able to follow the training they were offered.

(k) Women migrant workers

Women were more likely to report that they had not been given any induction training. They were also more likely to believe that their health, both physical and mental was being compromised by the work they were doing. And they were more likely to say that they had experienced discrimination at work.

In relation to pregnancy, women migrants faced particular problems. They had come to the UK to work and naturally were anxious not to have to stop working too early into the pregnancy. If they did become pregnant employers sometimes did not make adjustments to enable them to work safely and there was evidence of women compromising their health to continue in work.

(l) Knowledge and enforcement of health and safety rights

The migrant worker group expressed a low level of knowledge of their health and safety rights and of how to enforce them.

7.8 Summary

This chapter has considered migrant workers as an example of those workers who can suffer discrimination because they have a different ethnic origin or, maybe, skin colour to that of the host population. Those who are indigenous to a country but are in the minority because of their ethnic origin or colour also can suffer extensive discrimination.

It is interesting to look at the laws in the UK or elsewhere with regard to racial discrimination and speculate as to how much it has contributed to changing attitudes amongst the predominant white population. Matters have progressed significantly since overt expressions and advertising of racism was permitted, such as being able to select tenants for property by excluding people of colour or a certain nationality. The question is whether the law has really only suppressed these overt expressions or has contributed to a real change in attitudes.

Chapter 8

Religion or Belief

Chapter Contents

8.1 Introduction

This chapter is concerned with the protection offered by the law against discrimination on the grounds of religion or belief. This is one of the protected characteristics contained in section 4 of the Equality Act 2010. Clearly there is a close link between religion and the subject of Chapter 7 (race). It is also important to understand that the 'beliefs' protected may have nothing to do with religion or religious belief.

8.2 Religion

A question on religion was first asked in the 2001 census.[1] The publication of the 2011 census has allowed us to compare trends in religious belief over the ten-year period since then. Those who state an affiliation with the Christian religion remain the largest group at some 59 per cent (33.2 million) of residents in England and Wales. This is a decrease of 13 percentage points since 2001 when 72 per cent (37.3 million) of residents stated their religion as Christian. It is the only group to have experienced a decrease in numbers between 2001 and 2011 despite population growth.

The second largest category in 2011 was no religion. This increased 10 percentage points from 15 per cent (7.7 million) of residents in 2001, to 25 per cent (14.1 million) in 2011. The next most stated religion in England and Wales was Muslim with five per cent (2.7 million) of residents stating their religion as Muslim, an increase of two percentage points since 2001 when three per cent (1.5 million) of usual residents stated that they were Muslim.

The percentages reporting other religions are in shown in Table 8.1.

There is a difference between answering a question in the census that one is affiliated to a religion and actually participating in the practice and life of that religion. Some indication comes from the British Social Attitudes Survey 2010,[2] which asked questions about religion and participation.

Table 8.1 Religious affiliation in England and Wales 2001 and 2011

Religion	2001		2011		Change	
	Number	Per cent	Number	Per cent	Number	Percentage point
Christian	37,338	71.7	33,243	59.3	−4,095	−12.4
No religion	7,709	14.8	14,097	25.1	6,388	10.3
Muslim	1,547	3.0	2,706	4.8	1,159	1.8
Hindu	552	1.1	817	1.5	264	0.4
Sikh	329	0.6	423	0.8	94	0.2
Jewish	260	0.5	263	0.5	3	0.0
Buddhist	144	0.3	248	0.4	103	0.1
Other religion	151	0.3	241	0.4	90	0.1
Religion not stated	4,011	7.7	4,038	7.2	27	

1 See http://www.ons.gov.uk/ons/rel/census/2011-census/key-statistics-for-local-authorities-in-england-and-wales/stb-2011-census-key-statistics-for-england-and-wales.html#tab—Religion (last accessed 17 January 2013).
2 See http://ir2.flife.de/data/natcen-social-research/igb_html/index.php?bericht_id=1000001&index=&lang=ENG (last accessed May 2012); the chapter on religion is authored by Lucy Lee.

Half of the respondents did not regard themselves as belonging to a particular religion, whilst some 44% described themselves as Christian (Church of England 20%; Roman Catholic 9%; other Christian 15%). Some 64% of 18–24 year olds did not belong to a religion, compared to some 28% of those aged 65 and over. There has been a decline in religious affiliation over the years. In 1983 about 31% said that they did not belong to a religion compared to 50% in 2010. The biggest decline in affiliation concerned the Church of England, where it halved from 40% in 1983 to 20% in 2010.

Although formal legal protection did not appear in British law until the end of the twentieth century, there have traditionally been some attempts to accommodate religious belief and practice. Examples might be the fact that Sikhs are not required to wear crash helmets when using a motorcycle and that Jews and Muslims are exempted from law in relation to animal slaughter methods (Sandberg and Doe 2007). Such attempts to accommodate religious diversity are limited when the protection for religion and belief clashes with the protection offered to others, particularly the LGBT community.

Ill-treatment because of an individual's religion or religious belief can be closely connected to discrimination on the grounds of race or ethnicity. Sometimes the ill-treatment is the result of a lack of tolerance between different religious and/or ethnic groups and sometimes it is the result of oppression by the majority or ruling group who discriminate against an ethnic or religious minority. An example of the first of these is the conflict in Britain and elsewhere between Roman Catholic and Protestant branches of Christianity. The second is illustrated at its most extreme by the attempted extermination of Jewish people by Hitler's Germany in the twentieth century. It is important to recognise that the link between race and religion is not a simplistic one; for example, an estimated 43% of Muslims in the UK are of Pakistani origin, 6% are black and 11% white, whilst 97% of Christians and 97% of Jews are white (Bond et al. 2009).

Employment rates by ethnic origin in the UK are discussed in Chapter 7 on Race. There is some evidence, however, 'to suggest that religion does play a role in employment discrimination' (European Monitoring Centre on Racism and Xenophobia 2006). A report published by the European Monitoring Centre on Racism and Xenophobia (2006) gives two examples:

> For example, in the UK the BBC's Radio Five Live programme carried out an exercise where 50 firms received applications from six fictitious candidates with names strongly suggesting white British, African or Muslim background. The white candidates were more likely (25 per cent) than the black (13 per cent) applicants to be invited to interview, but those with a Muslim name (9 per cent) had the least success of all. In France in 2004 the Monitoring Centre on Discrimination at the University of Paris sent out different standard curricula vitae in response to 258 job advertisements for a sales person. It was found that a person from the Maghreb had five times less chance of getting a positive reply.

Research by the Equality and Human Rights Commission (2011c) in the UK showed that only 47% of Muslim men and 24% of Muslim women were employed. This compared to almost 80% of Christians and more than 80% of Hindus and Jews. There were particular issues for Muslim women and for young people; for example, some 13% of second-generation British Muslim women were unemployed, compared to 4% of second-generation Hindu and Sikh women. For young adults the report states that 'Muslims are also more likely to experience periods outside education, employment or training, than Christian young people or those of no religion'.

8.3 Belief

Belief means any religious or philosophical belief and also includes having a lack of belief.[3] According to the Code of Practice on Employment (EHRC 2011a), a belief that is not a religious belief may be a philosophical belief, such as Humanism and Atheism. A belief need not include faith or worship, but must affect how a person lives their life or perceives the world.

This approach was contained in the case of *Grainger plc v Nicholson*,[4] where a belief in man-made climate change was held to be a philosophical belief for the purposes of the legislation.[5] Mr Grainger was dismissed from his job. His employer claimed that it was on the grounds of redundancy, but Mr Grainger claimed that it was because of his belief that mankind was heading towards catastrophic climate change due to carbon emissions and that it was everyone's moral duty to live in a way that mitigated that change for future generations. He said that this belief affected the way that he lived his life including his choice of home, the way he travelled and what he ate and drank. The issue here was whether this amounted to a philosophical belief.

The Employment Appeal Tribunal stated that to be a belief that is protected by the legislation, the belief did not have to be something that governed the entirety of one's life. Examples given by the court were vegetarianism or pacifism. Both of these would be protected philosophical beliefs, so the belief did not have to be a fully-fledged system of thought. For a philosophical belief to be protected under the Act:

- it must be genuinely held;
- it must be a belief and not an opinion or viewpoint based on the present state of information available;
- it must be a belief as to a weighty and substantial aspect of human life and behaviour;
- it must attain a certain level of cogency, seriousness, cohesion and importance; and
- it must be worthy of respect in a democratic society, not incompatible with human dignity and not in conflict with the fundamental rights of others.[6]

8.4 The Equality Act 2010

The Framework Directive was transposed into national law by the Employment Equality (Religion or Belief) Regulations 2003,[7] and the Equality Act 2006 extended the protection outside the field of employment to include facilities, goods and services. These measures have now been absorbed into the Equality Act 2010. Section 4 of the Equality Act 2010 provides that religion or belief is one of the protected characteristics. The Equality Act 2010, as with the other protected characteristics, makes direct discrimination, indirect discrimination, harassment and victimisation on the characteristic of religion or belief unlawful. Religion means any religion and includes a lack of religion;[8] so, for example, devout Christians or Muslims are covered, but so are atheists. The Code of Practice on Employment states that the term 'religion' includes the more commonly recognised religions in the UK such as the Baha'i faith, Buddhism, Christianity, Hinduism, Islam, Jainism, Judaism, Rastafarianism, Sikhism and Zoroastrianism. Denominations or sects within religions, such as

---

3 Section 10(2) Equality Act 2010.
4 [2010] IRLR 4.
5 Much reliance is placed on Article 9 of the European Convention on Human Rights, which protects the right to freedom of thought, conscience and religion, and judicial decisions of the European Court of Human Rights.
6 See Code of Practice on Employment, para 2.59.
7 SI 2003/1660.
8 Section 10(1) Equality Act 2010.

Methodists within Christianity or Sunnis within Islam, may also be considered a religion for the purposes of the Act. The Code also provides that a religion need not be mainstream or well known to gain protection; however, it must have a clear structure and belief system. Ultimately it has been left to the courts to determine what constitutes a religion.

An example of how the courts approached the subject prior to regulation can be seen in the case of *Ahmad v Inner London Education Authority*.[9] This concerned a primary schoolteacher who was a devout Muslim, who required a short time off on Friday afternoons to attend prayers at a nearby mosque. When he was first employed in this post he had not told his employer of this need. The problem was that he could not get to the mosque and return without missing about forty-five minutes of his teaching. He had subsequently been offered employment on the basis of four and a half days a week, but he refused this and resigned, claiming unfair dismissal. The United Kingdom had not at the time incorporated the European Convention on Human Rights into national law, but, as Lord Denning stated in this case, 'we will do our best to see that our decisions are in conformity with it'. He then went on to say that such high-minded principles needed to be brought down to earth. The result was to reject the claim as it would give the Muslim community 'preferential treatment'. Referring to the Muslim community he stated that:

> If it should happen that, in the name of religious freedom, they would be given special privileges or advantages, it would provoke discontent, and even resentment among those with whom they work.

Lord Scarman dissented, stating that the application of such a rule would mean that any Muslim who took their religious duties seriously could never be employed on a full-time contract as a teacher. He said, in strong language, that:

> In modern British society, with its elaborate statutory protection of the individual from discrimination arising from race, colour, religion or sex, and against the background of the European Convention, this is unacceptable, inconsistent with the policy of modern statute law, and almost certainly a breach of our international obligations.

Lord Scarman, however, was in the minority when the court turned down Mr Ahmad's appeal. This is an old case and one must doubt whether the same decision would be reached today. It does, however, illustrate how it is possible to penalise someone for carrying out the activities and ritual connected to their religious beliefs.

How difficult it still is to deal with issues arising from this protection is well illustrated in the case of *Azmi*.[10] Mrs Azmi was a devout Muslim. Since the age of 15 she had worn a long dress (the *jabbah*) and usually wore a veil, which covered all her head and face except for her eyes, when in the presence of adult males. She was employed as a bilingual support worker (one of eight) working at a Church of England school controlled by the local authority. The school had approximately 530 children between the ages of 7 and 11 years. Some 92 per cent were Muslim of minority ethnic origin, mostly Indian and Pakistani. There were some 70 staff of whom 25 were Muslim and/or of minority ethnic origin. She impressed at her interview and had glowing references. She was offered the post and asked to work 20 hours per week and this was agreed. At her interview she did not indicate that her religious beliefs required her to wear a veil. It was during the first week of term that she asked if she could wear the veil when teaching with male teachers. The head teacher sought advice from the local authority, who stated that 'obscuring the face and mouth reduces the

---

9 [1977] ICR 490.
10 *Azmi v Kirklees Metropolitan Borough Council* [2007] IRLR 484.

non-verbal signals required between adult and pupil. In our view the desire to express religious identity does not overcome the primary requirement for optimal communication between adults and children'. Subsequently Mrs Azmi was asked not to wear her veil whilst teaching, but she continued to do so. Eventually her employment was suspended.

Mrs Azmi claimed, amongst other matters, both direct and indirect religious discrimination. She was unsuccessful in her claims. The direct discrimination claim was dismissed because the correct comparator (with whom she would need to show less favourable treatment) was a person who covered her face for a reason other than for a religious belief. It was clear that such a person would have been treated in the same way and not less favourably. The court accepted that, in relation to the claim for indirect discrimination, the provision, criterion or practice was apparently neutral and was likely to put persons of Mrs Azmi's belief at a disadvantage. It held, however, that it had been justified as a proportionate means of achieving a legitimate aim.

This is an illustration of how difficult such situations are and how limits on the protection from discrimination have to be balanced by the needs and rights of other groups in society. In this case it was the perceived needs of the children that took precedence. During the case there was much discussion about whether the wearing of the veil was a religious belief or was a manifestation of religious belief, although the court held that this was not a determinative issue.

8.5 Occupational requirements relating to organised religion and belief

The Equality Act 2010[11] provides that, in some circumstances, an employer may be permitted to require an applicant or employee to be of a particular sex or not to be a transsexual. There are also circumstances where the employer may be permitted to have rules with regard to marriage, civil partnership or sexual orientation.[12] The employer will need to show that:

(a)   the employment is for the purposes of an organised religion;

(b)   the application of the requirement engages the compliance or non-conflict principle; and

(c)   the person to whom A applies the requirement does not meet it (or A has reasonable grounds for not being satisfied that the person meets it).

The compliance principle relates to a requirement to comply with the doctrines of the religion in question; and the non-conflict principle relates to a requirement, because of the nature or context of employment, to avoid conflicting with strongly held religious views of a significant number of the religion's followers.[13] The Code of Practice on Employment gives some examples (at 13.12):

> An orthodox synagogue could apply a requirement for its rabbi to be a man.

> An evangelical church could require its ministers to be married or heterosexual if this enables the church to avoid a conflict with the strongly held religious convictions of its congregation.

According to the Code of Practice, the requirement must be a proportionate way of meeting the compliance or non-conflict principle and should only be used for a limited amount of positions, such as ministers of religion. It gives this example:

11   Schedule 9 Part 1.
12   Schedule 9 para 2(1); see also 13.12–13.18 Code of Practice on Employment.
13   Schedule 9 paras 2(5)–2(6).

The trustees of a Mosque want to employ two youth workers, one who will provide guidance on the teachings of the Koran and the other purely to organise sporting activities not involving promoting or representing the religion. The trustees apply an occupational requirement for both workers to be heterosexual. It might be lawful to apply the occupational requirement exception to the first post but not the second post because the second post does not engage the 'compliance' or the 'non-conflict' principle.

Additionally, an employer with an ethos based on religion or belief may be able to apply, in relation to work, a requirement to be of a particular religion or belief if that employer can show, having regard to that ethos and to the nature or context of the work, that:

(a)   it is an occupational requirement;

(b)   the application of the requirement is a proportionate means of achieving a legitimate aim; and

(c)   the person to whom the employer applies the requirement does not meet it (or the employer has reasonable grounds for not being satisfied that the person meets it).

The Code of Practice gives the example of a lawful exception, which might be a Humanist organisation that promotes Humanist philosophy and principles applying an occupational requirement for their chief executive to be a Humanist.

8.6 Manifestation of religious belief

There appears to be a distinction between the protection offered for being a member of a religious group and outward manifestations of religious belief. It is really an interesting question as to whether the law should intervene to protect people who, for example, wish to wear a symbol of their belief even though there might be offence caused to others who do not share that belief or, perhaps, who are totally opposed to that belief. It is here that one can perhaps see that there are limits to the protection offered by the law and it is of course a matter of debate as to where those limits should be. For now at least the courts have interpreted the law to distinguish between protecting the right to have a religious belief and the ability to manifest that belief through the wearing of particular symbols such as the Cross. This is shown clearly in *Eweida v British Airways plc*.[14]

Mrs Eweida was a devout Christian who regarded the Cross as the central image of her belief. She worked for British Airways as a member of their airport check-in staff. She wanted to wear a simple silver cross over her uniform so that it was in plain view. The company's rules only permitted the wearing of visible religious symbols where there was a 'mandatory' religious requirement. Mrs Eweida accepted that the wearing of the cross was not a mandatory requirement of her religion, but she wanted nevertheless to wear it as an expression of her faith. The problem arose partly because of a change in uniform style by British Airways. During the first few years of her employment the uniform included a high-necked blouse and she wore her cross under this when she wished to do so. The uniform was then changed to include an open-necked blouse, but also included the rule against the wearing of any visible item of adornment around the neck. Mrs Eweida came to work on a number of occasions wearing the cross visibly and was asked to cover it up, which at first she did. After she refused to do, so she was suspended from employment.

There was, of course, a great deal of publicity about the case and the Court of Appeal felt it necessary to say first what the case was not about, namely 'not about whether BA had adopted an

---

14 [2010] IRLR 322.

anti-Christian dress code, nor whether other religions were more favourably treated, nor whether BA had harassed the appellant because of her beliefs'. The Employment Tribunal had rejected the possibility of direct discrimination and the sole issue appealed was whether the company's policy resulted in unjustified indirect discrimination. Indeed, the company changed its policy and, from 2007, allowed the wearing of a faith or charity symbol with the uniform.

The Code of Practice on Employment points out that restrictions on some manifestations of belief may amount to indirect discrimination. Such manifestations could include the treating of certain days as days for worship or rest or the following of a particular dress code or diet. The Code provides an example:

> An employer has a 'no headwear' policy for its staff. Unless this policy can be objectively justi-fied, this will be indirect discrimination against Sikh men who wear the turban, Muslim women who wear a headscarf and observant Jewish men who wear a skullcap as manifestations of their religion.

In this case the Court of Appeal concluded that indirect discrimination had not been shown. The court stated that:

> Neither Mrs Eweida nor any witness on her behalf suggested that the visible wearing of a cross was more than a personal preference on her part. There was no suggestion that her religious belief, however profound, called for it.

There have been a number of cases decided concerning the wearing of religious symbols and dress in schools that are relevant to this issue, such as that of *Watkins-Singh*.[15] These cases are not just about protecting a person's religious beliefs but also about discrimination on the basis of ethnic origin. They are dealt with in Chapter 7 on race, but the *Watkins-Singh* case is discussed here because it also deals with the wearing of a particular religious symbol. The case concerned the refusal of a school to allow a Sikh girl to wear the Kara, which is a thin steel bangle. The Kara is very important to Sikhs as a visible sign of their identity and faith. As explained in the case, the Kara is one of the five visible symbols that Sikhs are instructed to adopt. One of the issues was whether the refusal by the school to allow the wearing of the Kara amounted to unjustifiable indirect discrimination on the grounds of both race and religion or belief. In *Mandla v Dowell Lee*[16] the House of Lords had accepted that Sikhs were a racial group for the purposes of the Race Relations Act 1976. It was also accepted that a person could be a Sikh by religion as well as race. The court distinguished other cases brought under Article 9 of the European Convention on Human Rights (see below) where the decision was that the banning of wearing a *niqab* (veil covering the face) or a *jihab* (long coat-like garment) could be justified. In contrast the Kara was much less visible and 'unostentatious'. The court decided that not granting permission to wear the Kara did amount to indirect racial and religious discrimina-tion. This was because of two factors:

> The wearing of the article is a matter of *exceptional* importance as an expression of her race and culture. The second factor is the unobtrusive nature of the Kara being 50 mm wide and made of plain steel.

According to the court, any fear that this would make inroads into the school's dress code with many other girls wearing items to show their nationality or other beliefs, were unjustified.

---

15 *The Queen on the application of Sarika Angel Watkins-Singh v The Governing Body of Aberdare Girls' High School and Rhondda Cynon Taf Unitary Authority* [2008] EWHC 1865 (Admin) Case no. CO/11435/2007.
16 [1983] IRLR 209.

8.7 Sexual orientation

The issue about making exceptions to the principle of non-discrimination comes to the fore when considering the potential clash with the protected characteristic of sexual orientation (see Chapter 10). Some religions or parts of religions will not accept same sex relationships, yet LGBT people have the right not to be discriminated against on the grounds of their sexuality. There are some cases that illustrate the difficulty experienced by both people with strong religious beliefs and homosexual people.

Ladele v London Borough of Islington[17] concerned a registrar of births deaths and marriages who was a strongly committed Christian. She believed that marriage was a lifetime arrangement between a man and a woman. As a result of the Civil Partnership Act 2004, which came into effect in December 2005, same sex couples were able to enter into civil partnerships. Mrs Ladele thought that this effectively allowed same sex couples to marry and she thought that such same sex marriages were contrary to God's law and were sinful. She made it clear that she would be unhappy at conducting civil partnership registrations, but her manager believed that they should be shared out amongst all the registrars. As a compromise she was offered the chance of only conducting registrations that consisted of completing forms. It emerged that a Muslim working in another Borough had found such an arrangement acceptable, but Mrs Ladele did not. She wrote to the council asking that her beliefs be accommodated. She avoided civil partnership ceremonies by swopping rosters with colleagues and the Council's management tolerated this arrangement. Two gay registrars, however, objected and alleged that she was in breach of the Council's anti-discrimination policies and that they felt victimised by her refusal. Eventually disciplinary proceedings were started against her. The outcome was to tell her that she must take civil partnership events but that the original compromise arrangement could hold. She brought proceedings alleging direct and indirect discrimination and harassment based upon her religious beliefs.

The Employment Tribunal upheld all her complaints. The refusal to allow her to opt out of civil partnerships amounted to direct discrimination. The EAT reversed this and said that this did not amount to direct discrimination as all registrars were treated in the same way. The court held that 'Mrs Ladele's objection was based on her view of marriage, which was not a core part of her religion; and Islington's requirement in no way prevented her from worshipping as she wished'.[18] The reality was that she wanted to be treated differently than everyone else. It was a complaint about a failure to accommodate her difference rather than a complaint that she was being discriminated against because of that difference.

Similarly the case of *McClintock*[19] concerned a magistrate who was a member of the Family Panel. He felt that his religious and philosophical beliefs would not enable him to place children with same sex couples. This was something that was likely to occur during his work on the Family Panel. He wanted to be excused from such cases, but his request to be an exception was refused, so he resigned and brought proceedings stating that he had been indirectly discriminated against. The EAT dismissed his claim because it felt that his objection was not based upon any religious or philosophical belief; it was not enough to have an opinion based upon some real or perceived logic.

A further case that followed the *Ladele* decision was that of *McFarlane*.[20] The complainant was a Christian who believed that homosexual activity was a sin. He was a counsellor for an organisation that provided relationship counselling services and which was a member of the British Association for Sexual and Relationship Therapy, which had a Code of Ethics that required the therapist to avoid

---

17 *Ladele v LB Islington* [2010] IRLR 211.
18 Para 52 of the judgment.
19 *McClintock v Department of Constitutional Affairs* [2008] IRLR 29.
20 *McFarlane v Relate Avon Ltd* [2010] IRLR 872.

discrimination on the grounds of sexual orientation. When recruited he was obliged to sign up to the equal opportunities policy, which provided that no one should receive less favourable treatment on the basis of various characteristics including sexual orientation. He had no problems counselling same sex couples when there were no sexual issues. He asked to be exempted from such counselling when there were. This request was refused and eventually he was dismissed for gross misconduct. The dismissal letter stated that 'on 7 January 2008 you stated to Relate that you would comply with its equal opportunities policy and professional ethics policy in relation to work with same-sex couples and same-sex activities, when you had no intention of complying with Relate's policies on those issues'.

The court followed the decision in *Ladele*, but also said that there was a need to distinguish between the law's protection of the right to hold and express a belief and the law's protection of that belief's substance or content. Laws LJ stated further that:

> The common law and ECHR [European Convention of Human Rights] Article 9 offer vigorous protection of the Christian's right (and every other person's right) to hold and express his or her beliefs. And so they should. By contrast they do not, and should not, offer any protection whatever of the substance or content of those beliefs on the ground only that they are based on religious precepts. These are twin conditions of a free society.

So the law is a defender of the right to hold and express beliefs, but does not have the role of protecting the beliefs themselves.

8.8 The European Convention on Human Rights

Copsey v Devon Clays[21] is a good example of how the courts deal with the dilemma of protecting individual freedoms within the context of the needs of a wider society. Mr Copsey was a Christian employee whose sincerity, according to the Court of Appeal, was not in question. He sought to manifest his religious beliefs by observing Sunday as a day of rest in accordance with the Fourth Commandment.[22] This meant refusing to work on Sundays. His employer operated clay quarries in Devon. They progressively took on extra work and eventually changed relevant employees' working hours to a seven-day shift system. My Copsey's refusal to work on Sundays made it impossible for him to accept this arrangement and eventually he was dismissed. Although this was really a case about unfair dismissal, rather than direct or indirect discrimination, the court did consider issues related to Article 9 of the European Convention on Human Rights.

Article 9, as transposed by the Human Rights Act 1998, states that:

1. Everyone has the right to freedom of thought, conscience and religion; this right includes freedom to change his religion or belief and freedom, either alone or in community with others and in public and in private, to manifest his religion or belief, in worship, teaching, practice and observance.
2. Freedom to manifest one's religion or beliefs shall be subject only to such limitations as are prescribed by law and are necessary in a democratic society in the interests of public safety, for the protection of public order, health or morals, or for the protection of the rights and freedoms of others.

---

21 *Stephen Copsey v WWB Devon Clays Ltd* [2005] EWCA Civ 932.
22 Exodus, Chapter 20.

The Code of Practice on Employment points out that whilst Article 9 gives people an absolute right to hold a particular religion or belief, the right to manifest that belief is qualified and, in certain circumstances, may be limited. It needs to be balanced against other Convention rights such as the right to respect for family life (Article 8) or the right to freedom of expression (Article 10). The Code (at 2.61) says that there is not always a clear dividing line between holding a religion or belief and manifesting that religion or belief. Limits on the right to manifest religion or belief may, however, amount to indirect discrimination.

The Court of Appeal in *Copsey* cited the case of *Kokkinakis v Greece*[23] at the European Court of Human Rights. In this case the Court had considered Article 9 and the limitations to the protection offered. It stated that the limitations in Article 9 only referred to the freedom to manifest one's religion or belief and that:

> It recognises that in democratic societies, in which several religions coexist within one and the same population, it may be necessary to place restrictions on this freedom in order to reconcile the interests of the various groups and ensure that everyone's beliefs are respected.

Both the Employment Tribunal and the Employment Appeal Tribunal had concluded that Mr Copsey's dismissal was for 'some other substantial reason'[24] because he would not work the seven-day shift pattern and not because of his religious beliefs. The Court of Appeal, however, stated that there was a connection between his dismissal and his religious beliefs. Thus Article 9 of the Convention was engaged. The court went on to review the approach of the European Court of Human Rights, which had consistently concluded that Article 9 is not engaged when there is a conflict between working hours and the employee's religious beliefs. This was because the employee was always free to resign if he or she wanted to manifest his or her beliefs. This somewhat hard-hearted approach was exemplified in the following cases at the European Court of Human Rights:

- *Ahmad v United Kingdom*[25] concerned a devout Muslim who wanted time off from teaching to attend a nearby mosque on Fridays. This was refused and he was forced to resign. The local education authority was entitled to rely on its contract with the employee and that, throughout his employment, he remained free to resign if and when his teaching obligations conflicted with his religious duties.
- *Kontinnen v Finland*[26] concerned a civil servant who was a Seventh-Day Adventist, who was dismissed because he refused to work after dusk on Fridays. Again there was a distinction between fulfilling a contract of employment and the freedom to manifest religious beliefs. The applicant was always free to give up his post and that this was the 'ultimate guarantee of his right to freedom of religion'.

The Court of Appeal also referred to *Stedman v United Kingdom*,[27] where there was a similar outcome for an applicant who did not wish to work on Sundays.

Although the Court of Appeal was clearly unhappy at this approach, it was obliged to adopt it and find that Mr Copsey's dismissal did not engage Article 9. Lord Justice Mummery stated that:

---

23 (1993) 17 EHRR 397 at 419.
24 See Section 94 Employment Rights Act 1996.
25 (1981) 4 EHRR 128. See *Ahmad v Inner London Education Authority* [1977] ICR 490 discussed above.
26 [1996] App no 249/49/94.3.
27 (1997) 23 EHHR CD168.

My own view, for what it is worth, is that in some sections of the Community this is a controversial question which will not go away and that its resolution requires a political solution following full consultation between government, leaders of employers and trades unions, and religious leaders.

8.9 The European Court of Human Rights

In September 2012 the European Court of Human Rights heard an appeal concerning a number of UK cases[28] with regard to the issues concerning a right to manifest ones religious beliefs and the clash with protection on the grounds of sexual orientation. The following is a summary from the Court's announcement of the cases.

All four applicants are practising Christians who complain that UK law did not sufficiently protect their rights to freedom of religion and freedom from discrimination at work. Ms Eweida, a British Airways employee, and Ms Chaplin, a geriatrics nurse, complain that their employers placed restrictions on their visibly wearing Christian crosses around their necks while at work. Ms Ladele, a Registrar of Births, Deaths and Marriages, and Mr McFarlane, a Relate counsellor, complain about their dismissal for refusing to carry out certain of their duties which they considered would condone homosexuality. The Court's notice of the case summed them up as follows:

Chaplin and Eweida

Both applicants believe that the visible wearing of a cross is an important part of the manifestation of their faith.

Both applicants lodged claims with the Employment Tribunal complaining in particular of discrimination on religious grounds. The Tribunal rejected Ms Eweida's claim, finding that the visible wearing of a cross was not a requirement of the Christian faith but the applicant's personal choice and that she had failed to establish that British Airways' uniform policy had put Christians in general at a disadvantage. Her appeal to the Court of Appeal was also subsequently rejected and the Supreme Court refused her leave to appeal in May 2010. Ms Chaplin's claim was also rejected in May 2010, the Tribunal holding that the hospital's position had been based on health and safety rather than religious grounds and that there was no evidence that anyone other than the applicant had been put at particular disadvantage. Given the Court of Appeal's decision in Ms Eweida's case, Ms Chaplin was advised that an appeal on points of law had no prospect of success.

Ladele and McFarlane

Both Ms Ladele and Mr McFarlane are Christians, who believe that homosexual relationships are contrary to God's law and that it is incompatible with their beliefs to do anything to condone homosexuality.

Both applicants brought proceedings before the Employment Tribunal on grounds of religious discrimination; Mr McFarlane also claimed that he had been unfairly and wrongfully dismissed.

---

28 *Chaplin v the United Kingdom* (application no. 59842/10); *Eweida v the United Kingdom* (no. 48420/10); *Ladele v the United Kingdom* (no. 51671/10); *McFarlane v the United Kingdom* (no. 36516/10).

Both claims were rejected on appeal on the basis that their employers were not only entitled to require them to carry out their duties but also to refuse to accommodate views which contradicted their fundamental declared principles – and, all the more so, where these principles were required by law, notably under the Equality Act (Sexual Orientation) Regulations 2007. Ultimately, in March 2010 Ms Ladele was refused leave to appeal to the Supreme Court and, in April 2010, Mr McFarlane was refused permission to appeal again to the Employment Appeal Tribunal as there was no realistic prospect of it succeeding, given that Mr McFarlane's case could not sensibly be distinguished from Ms Ladele's.

The Court the summed up their complaint as:

> Relying in particular on Articles 9 (freedom of religion) and 14 (prohibition of discrimination), all four applicants complain that domestic law failed to adequately protect their right to manifest their religion.

The Court's judgment was announced in January 2013. Ms Eweida's claim was upheld but the other three failed. In both the Eweida case and the Chaplin case the Court stated that there had been an interference with their right to manifest their religion in that they had been unable to wear their crosses visibly at work. The courts in the UK had attempted to balance the right of individuals to manifest their religious belief against employers' policies that restricted this right. In Ms Eweida's case the requirements of British Airway's uniform policy were not sufficient to outweigh this right. Indeed, British Airways had subsequently changed its policy and allowed such symbols to be worn, showing that it had been possible all along. In Ms Chaplin's case, however, the demands of health and safety outweighed the right. She was a nurse working on a ward and there was a potential danger to herself and patients from wearing the cross.

The Court appeared less sympathetic to Ms Ladele and Mr McFarlane, stating that:

> The Court considered that the most important factor to be taken into account was that the policies of the applicants' employers – to promote equal opportunities and to require employees to act in a way which did not discriminate against others – had the legitimate aim of securing the rights of others, such as same sex couples, which were also protected under the Convention.

The authorities had wide discretion when striking a balance between the employers' right to secure the rights of others and the applicants' right to manifest their religion. In the cases of Ladele and McFarlane the Court concluded that the British authorities had struck the right balance.

8.10 Summary

This area of law is not only about the clash between the protected characteristics of religion or belief and sexual orientation, although this is important. It is also about recognising the diversity of faith in the United Kingdom and ensuring, as far as possible, that individuals and groups are able to freely believe in and practice their religions and religious beliefs.

Perhaps the area where there is a clash is in the manifestation of one's beliefs or religion, as this is where different beliefs and practices may coincide and it is this that makes the Chaplin and Eweida decisions important. In a sense the clash between the protected characteristics of sexual orientation and religion is also about the boundaries and how far one needs to compromise in order to maximise the protection for those who welcome homosexuality and those who disapprove of it. The *Ladele* and *McFarlane* cases show that it is difficult to strike the right balance, but it is likely to be unusual to be able to restrict the rights of same sex couples just because one person has a personal belief that homosexuality is wrong.

Chapter 9

Sex Equality

Chapter Contents

9.1 Introduction

In this chapter we consider a number of important issues related to the protected characteristics of sex and marriage/civil partnership. We also consider the subject of equal pay or 'equality of terms'. This perhaps shows the limits of the law, when one considers that while in the UK there has been some sex discrimination legislation since the 1960s and both the Sex Discrimination Act and the Equal Pay Act came into effect as long ago as 1975, discrimination and inequality continue.

9.2 Women and men

Although the Equality Act 2010 has, as one primary purpose, the removing of gender imbalances between men and women, it does not necessarily require the same treatment as between men and women. The aim is to ensure that one gender is not treated less favourably than another. An example of this can be seen in complaints concerning the differences in dress codes between the sexes. In *Smith v Safeway plc*,[1] for example, a male employee was dismissed because his ponytail grew too long to keep under his hat. The store had a code that required men to have hair not below shirt collar level, but female employees were permitted to have hair down to shoulder length. The court held that the employer was imposing a dress code that reflected a conventional outlook and that this should not be held to be discriminatory. The effect of such a decision was, however, that a male employee was dismissed because of the length of his hair, which would have been permissible in a female employee.[2]

Section 11(a) of the Equality Act 2010 also makes it clear that this characteristic applies to men as well as women. An example of this occurred in *Eversheds v De Belin*.[3] The employer in this case was in a difficult situation. The claimant was one of two solicitors of whom one was to be made redundant. The choice for the employer was between the claimant, who was a man, and another solicitor who was absent on maternity leave at the time. The employer adopted a points scheme to decide on which person was to go. One of the factors in gaining points was called 'lock up'. This was the amount of time between undertaking a piece of work and receiving payment. The claimant was scored on his actual performance, but the person absent on maternity leave was given the maximum possible points for lock up, even though she did not have any payments during the chosen period. This enabled her to gain marginally more points than the claimant and so he was the one made redundant. As a result he made a claim for sex discrimination and unfair dismissal. Given the restrictions on acting against pregnant women or people on maternity leave, the employer argued that they had fulfilled their responsibility to the employee on maternity leave. The EAT held, in the event, that the law that gave pregnant women and those on maternity leave special treatment and protection still required the treatment to be a proportionate means of achieving a legitimate aim. In this case the treatment given to the absent employee was disproportionate and amounted to direct sex discrimination against the male employee.[4]

Women are less likely than men to be working full time and at all ages there exists a gender pay gap in favour of men. Part-time work is often low-paid work. The size of the pay gap depends upon what formula one uses, but the Fawcett Society estimates it to be some 14.9 per cent.[5] Although there has been a steady decline in the full-time pay gap over the years, its existence remains stubbornly

1 See *Smith v Safeway plc* [1996] IRLR 457.
2 In *Burrett v West Birmingham Health Authority* [1994] IRLR 7 female nurses were required to wear caps but male nurses were not. The EAT held that the important issue was that they both had to wear uniforms, not that those uniforms differed. See also *Department for Work & Pensions v Thompson* [2004] IRLR 348.
3 *Eversheds Legal Services Ltd v De Belin* [2011] IRLR 448.
4 *Nelson v Newry and Mourne DC* [2009] IRLR 548 was also a case where a man claimed direct sex discrimination. This case concerned two council employees, one male and one female, who were investigated for misusing council property. They were treated in different ways with regard to the disciplinary process and the man was given a much more severe sanction than the female.
5 See http://www.fawcettsociety.org.uk/index.asp?PageID=321 (last accessed 17 January 2013).

persistent. The part-time gap (i.e. comparing the wages of part-time women workers to those of full-time male workers) has remained fairly constant.[6] These figures hide some striking extremes; for example the Equality and Human Rights Commission reported that men received bonus payments in the City (of London) at a rate that was five times the amount received by women.[7] The result was that women earned 87.4 per cent of the rate earned by men using the median figure, and 82.8 per cent using the mean.

Women also suffer in comparison to men in other ways. For example, a BIS report (BIS 2011) provides the following information, from research carried out by Cranfield University about women and membership of the boards of companies in the FTSE 100:

- there are 141 women holding 163 FTSE 100 board seats (out of 1,086 board positions);
- there are 20 (6.6 per cent) female executive directorships and 143 (22.4 per cent) female non-executive directorships;
- the number of companies with no women on the board has dropped to 11 from 21;
- the number of companies with more than one woman on the board has increased to 50; and
- of the 47 new female appointments, 29 of the women (62 per cent) have had no prior FTSE board experience.

Although matters were improving, there was a long way to go before any equality between men and women could be achieved. Indeed, it has been reported that the European Commission may try to introduce legislation to ensure that the membership of the boards of listed companies should be at least 40 per cent female by 2020 (Fontanella-Khan 2012). It seems unlikely that such a policy will be successful.

Stereotypes of women are common and influence the role that women play in society; for example, women are seen as natural carers for children and older people and this can influence the way that their role at work is perceived by others and themselves. B v A[8] was a case where a man complained that he had suffered as a result of gender stereotyping. The case concerned an executive in a local authority who claimed that she had been raped by a colleague and that this was the culmination of a period of sexual harassment. She did not make a formal complaint to the police, but the CEO dismissed the alleged rapist. Subsequently the police decided not to take further action, so he made a complaint of sex discrimination, amongst other matters, namely that the employer had been motivated by a gender stereotype that a complaint by a woman against a man for rape had to be well founded. The ET rejected this, but still found sex discrimination because the employer had not gone through any form of due process. The EAT overturned the decision and held that the CEO had been motivated by a fear of further violence towards the claimant; however, the EAT said that this was not necessarily due to gender stereotyping. He would have acted in the same way if the alleged attacker had been a woman and the victim a man, so there was no case for less favourable treatment.

9.3 The European Union

The Equal Opportunities and Equal Treatment Directive[9] provides, in Article 1, that its purpose is:

---

6 See EHRC 2011c.
7 See BBC news website 6 September 2009, www.bbc.co.uk.
8 [2010] IRLR 400.
9 Directive 2006/54/EC on the implementation of the principle of equal opportunities and equal treatment of men and women in matters of employment and occupation OJ L204/23 26.7.2006. This Directive recast seven previous sex equality Directives, including the Equal Pay Directive 75/117, the Equal Treatment Directive 76/207 as amended by Directive 2002/73 and the Burden of Proof Directive 97/80, into one consolidated Directive from 15 August 2009, although the consolidated Directive itself had to be transposed into national law by 15 August 2008.

to ensure the implementation of the principle of equal opportunities and equal treatment of men and women in matters of employment and occupation.

Article 2 states that, for the purposes of this Directive, discrimination includes:

- harassment and sexual harassment, as well as any less favourable treatment based on a person's rejection of or submission to such conduct;
- instruction to discriminate against persons on grounds of sex; and
- any less favourable treatment of a woman related to pregnancy or maternity leave within the meaning of Directive 92/85/EC.

The extent to which the social objectives of Article 157 TFEU (141 EC) and, consequently, the Equal Treatment Directives could influence the development of equal opportunities has been considered by the Court of Justice. In *Marschall*[10] the complainant was a male comprehensive schoolteacher who had applied for promotion to a higher grade. He was told that an equally qualified female applicant would be given the position as there were fewer women than men at the more senior grade. The Court considered previous judgments,[11] which concluded that the Equal Treatment Directive did not permit national rules that enabled automatic priority to be given to female applicants for a job. There was a distinction between those measures that were designed to remove obstacles to women in employment and those measures that constituted positive discrimination by giving them preference just because they were women. This latter approach conflicted with the Equal Treatment Directive. Equality is to be achieved by equality of opportunity rather than equality of outcomes (see Chapter 1). This still seems to be the situation even though Article 157(4) of the TFEU states:

> With a view to ensuring full equality of practice between men and women in working life, the principle of equal treatment shall not prevent any Member State from maintaining or adopting measures for providing for specific advantages in order to make it easier for the under-represented sex to pursue a vocational activity or to prevent or compensate for disadvantages in professional careers.

In *Abrahamsson and Anderson v Fogelqvist*[12] the Court of Justice stated that this approach did not allow positive discrimination in favour of women in the selection process. There needed to be an objective assessment of the qualifications of the man and woman competing for the job in question to ensure that they were similar before any preference could be given to the woman as a result of women being under-represented in the workforce.[13]

Article 3 of the Equal Opportunities and Equal Treatment Directive now states simply that:

> Member States may maintain or adopt measures within the meaning of Article 157(4) of the Treaty with a view to ensuring full equality in practice between men and women in working life.

9.4 The Equality Act 2010

Sex is one of the nine protected characteristics in the Equality Act 2010; thus direct discrimination, indirect discrimination, harassment and victimisation because of sex are made unlawful. There can

---

10 Case C-409/95 *Marschall v Land Nordrhein-Westfalen* [1998] IRLR 39.
11 See, for example, Case C-450/93 *Kalanke v Freie Hansestadt Bremen* [1995] ECR 660.
12 Case 407/98 *Abrahamsson and Anderson v Fogelqvist* [2000] IRLR 732.
13 See Case 158/97 *Application by Badeck* [2000] IRLR 432.

be no justification for direct discrimination in situations related to the protected characteristic of sex, but a comparative approach is still required. It needs to be shown that the woman (or man) has received less favourable treatment than the comparator of the opposite sex. The complainant needs to be able to prove facts from which the Employment Tribunal could conclude without an adequate explanation that the respondent had committed an act of discrimination. An example of this can be seen in *Hewage v Grampian Health Board*,[14] where a female Sri Lankan-born hospital consultant was able to show that she had been treated differently to white male consultants. This case is useful because the Supreme Court here discusses the approach to the two-stage test for applying the statutory provisions set out in *Igen v Wong*[15] and applied in *Madarassy*.[16]

Indirect discrimination (section 19) results from the equal implementation of neutral rules that end up causing a disproportionate disadvantage to a particular group of people (in this case those of a particular sex) coming within one of the protected grounds, for which there no objective justification can be shown. Thus it occurs when a policy (provision, criterion or practice) that applies in the same way for everybody has an effect that particularly disadvantages people with a protected characteristic. Where a particular group is disadvantaged in this way, a person in that group is indirectly discriminated against if he or she is put at a disadvantage, unless A can show that it is a proportionate (appropriate and necessary) means of achieving a legitimate aim (section 19(2) (d)). Each situation needs to be looked at on its own merits. In the past a 'requirement or condition' (provision, criterion or practice) has included, for example, the necessity for previous management training or supervisory experience,[17] a contractual requirement for employees to serve in any part of the United Kingdom at the employer's discretion[18] or the imposition of new rostering arrangements for train drivers.[19]

Indirect discrimination applies to all the protected characteristics except for pregnancy and maternity.

9.4.1 Sexual harassment

Sexual harassment occurs when there is unwanted conduct of a sexual nature that has the effect of violating a person's dignity or creating an intimidating, hostile, degrading, humiliating or offensive environment for the complainant (section 26(2) Equality Act 2010). It also occurs when a worker is treated less favourably by their employer because the worker submitted to, or rejected, unwanted conduct of a sexual nature, or unwanted conduct that is related to sex or gender reassignment, and the unwanted conduct has any of the effects mentioned (section 26(3) Equality Act 2010). The Code of Practice on Employment (EHRC 2011a) gives a simple example:

> A shopkeeper propositions one of his shop assistants. She rejects his advances and then is turned down for a promotion which she believes she would have got if she had accepted her boss's advances. The shop assistant would have a claim for harassment.

Section 26(3)(a) of the Equality Act 2010 refers to unwanted conduct by 'A or another person' and the Code of Practice on Employment gives a further example of this:

---

14 [2012] IRLR 870.
15 [2005] IRLR 258.
16 *Madarassy v Nomura International plc* [2007] IRLR 246.
17 *Falkirk City Council v Whyte* [1997] IRLR 560.
18 *Meade-Hill and National Union of Civil and Public Servants v British Council* [1995] IRLR 478.
19 *London Underground v Edwards* [1998] IRLR 364.

A female worker is asked out by her team leader and she refuses. The team leader feels resentful and informs the Head of Division about the rejection. The Head of Division subsequently fails to give the female worker the promotion she applies for, even though she is the best candidate. She knows that the team leader and the Head of Division are good friends and believes that her refusal to go out with the team leader influenced the Head of Division's decision. She could have a claim of harassment over the Head of Division's actions.

The conduct needs to have the 'purpose' or 'effect' of creating the unwanted conditions, so even if the purpose of the action is not to harass, it can be still be harassment if it has that effect. The Code of Practice on Employment provides the example of male employees looking at pornography on their computers. The purpose may not be to harass female colleagues, but it might have that effect.

9.5 Marriage or civil partnership

Marriage or civil partnership is also a protected characteristic under the Equality Act 2010. Civil partnerships are considered further in Chapter 10, which is concerned with sexual orientation.

The characteristic applies to those who are married or in a civil partnership, so just living together is not enough. This may be a rule originally designed to stop discrimination against married women in employment, although it also applies to men. However, there is no corresponding rule that states that it is unlawful to discriminate against people because they are unmarried or not in a civil partnership.

It appears that it is the fact of being married (or in a civil partnership) that is important. In *Hawkins v Atex Group Ltd*[20] the complainant was dismissed because she was married to the company chief executive, which was not in accord with the company's policy. The EAT, however, held that she was not dismissed because of the fact that she was married, but because she was married to the Executive Officer. Someone who was not married, but in a so-called 'common law marriage' with the CEO, would also have been dismissed in this situation. It seems a narrow view of the protection offered by the legislation. The protection is available based on the fact of marriage, rather than based on being married to a particular person. This contrasts with the view in *Dunn v Institute of Cemetery and Crematorium Management*[21] where the EAT held that:

> A person who is married or who is in a civil partnership is protected against discrimination on the ground of that relationship and on the ground of their relationship to the other partner.[22]

Thus this case concluded that the fact of marriage to a specific person was also protected by the legislation. This and previous cases had been brought under the Sex Discrimination Act 1975 to show that the treatment of married women was a sex discrimination issue. In *Coleman v Sky Oceanic Ltd*,[23] for example, two competing travel firms employed one member each of what became a married couple. There was a concern about confidentiality of each business's information. The two companies consulted and decided to dismiss the female because the man was assumed to be the breadwinner. Such an assumption, according to the Court of Appeal, was an assumption based upon sex.[24]

---

20 [2012] IRLR 807.
21 [2012] All ER (D) 173.
22 Para 41. The court relied on the decision in *Chief Constable of Bedfordshire v Graham* [2002] IRLR 239.
23 [1981] IRLR 398 CA. On assumed ethnic characteristics see *Bradford NHS Trust v Al-Shahib* [2003] IRLR 4.
24 See also *Chief Constable of the Bedfordshire Constabulary v Graham* [2002] IRLR 239.

9.6 Older women

As an example of the particular disadvantage that women can suffer, we here look at the position of older women and the disadvantages they suffer, particularly in relation to their rights to pensions. The position of older women was summarised in an EIRO report (EIRO 2009) as:

- Older women workers represent an increasing proportion of the workforce in the European Union, especially in the 55–64 years age group. Employment rates for older women workers have been increasing in Europe.
- Older women workers tend to work part time and a higher proportion are on temporary contracts.
- Women aged 55 years and over are much more likely to be working on insecure contracts than men of the same age.
- The gender pay gap still exists for both older and younger women workers.
- Women are still concentrated in certain occupational groups, such as care workers, clerical workers and service and sales workers.
- The likelihood of a woman being a boss is highest in the 55+ age group.
- Older women are more likely than men to play a dual role of both working and caring, if there are care responsibilities in the family.
- Only a small proportion of companies pay specific attention to gender and there is little evidence that gender considerations have become more prominent over time. However, with the rise in the employment rate of older women workers, some companies have introduced specific policies to improve the working life of their older women workers and increase their level of recruitment.
- Women are still retiring earlier than their male colleagues. But this situation may change in incoming years with the growing need to keep older people in the workforce longer.

Generally older women may suffer from age and sex discrimination separately or combined into prejudice against older women. A good example is the case of Miriam O'Reilly and the BBC.[25] Ms O'Reilly was a presenter who claimed that she had suffered from being an older woman in the BBC. Something of the attitudes in the media were revealed in the Employment Tribunal, which cited examples of comments from colleagues such as how she would need to look out for her wrinkles once high definition TV came in, or that it was time for Botox, or whether she could not be used for prime time because she would not pass the young and pretty test. She was successful in her claim for age discrimination, but these comments are ones that are most likely to be made against older women.

The disadvantages that older women suffer need to be looked at from a lifetime perspective. Over a lifetime women are more likely to suffer disadvantage in employment compared to men. This can be the result of having children, being a carer for children or older people, working part time, making fewer pension contributions and so on. A report called Implementing Equality for Older People (2004) published by the Equality Authority in Ireland stated:

> Older peoples' experiences have been acquired through living within a particular set of social, economic and cultural circumstances. So, the experience of an older professional man can be quite different from the experience of an older woman in the home. Within the group of older people, there are people who suffer and/or have suffered discrimination on other grounds. The discrimination problems faced by the current generation of older women largely arise from

---

25 Miriam O'Reilly v BBC Case Number: 2200423/2010 (2011).

past discrimination on the grounds of gender, in particular exclusion from the labour market, arising from the 'marriage bar' and caring responsibilities, and the consequent exclusion from independent pension arrangements.

Older women may suffer from more disadvantages than older men because they tend to live longer, although the life expectancy gap between the sexes has narrowed in recent years. There were 28 per cent more women than men over the age of 50 years in 1961. This difference had narrowed to 18 per cent in 2002. Projections suggest a further narrowing with the difference in numbers being reduced to 14 per cent by 2031 (Office for National Statistics 2004). Older women are often poorer because of this relative longevity and for a number of other reasons, which may include the fact that women on average receive a much lower occupational pension income partly because they were dependent upon male pension-holding partners and because many will take career breaks to care for children and elders. The result of this is that, on average, womens' income during their lifetime is some £250,000 less than mens', with an income in retirement that is some 57 per cent of men's (Age Reference Group 2005). Lower overall employment meant fewer opportunities to accrue pension rights; and until the early 1990s part-time employment very rarely involved pension scheme membership (Pensions Commission 2004).

In the United Kingdom research has also shown that, taking all forms of inactivity together, the chances of men leaving inactivity for paid work were sharply reduced after the age of 50 years 'and were close to zero for those over 60'. For women the chances of moving out of inactivity were much reduced after the age of 40 years and 'was particularly uncommon for those older than their late 50s' (McKay and Middleton 1998). Older women are more likely not to be in paid employment. In the United Kingdom some 26 per cent of all women between 16 and state pension age are economically inactive, compared to 17 per cent of men.[26]

Older women are more likely to work part time and, as a result, have lower average earnings. Figures published by the European Commission show that this is a pattern of employment that is continuing. In 2009 some 31 per cent of employed women in the EU27 worked part time, compared with just 8 per cent of male workers (European Commission 2010). However, these figures hide differences related to age and gender. One report (European Commission 2004) concluded:

> There is a clear gender distinction in the occurrence of part-time work by age. In general, men are most likely to be in part-time employment during their youth, while for women it is during the latter stages of their working lives. Furthermore, while the share of part-time employment for men decreases sharply from youth to prime age, for women the share remains roughly the same across these age categories.

It is also true that women are more likely to suffer age discrimination at a younger age than men. Women are traditionally perceived as being 'older' at a much younger age than men and a greater proportion are therefore likely to suffer from age discrimination related to their sex. One survey showed a respondent employer stating that women who returned to work in their mid-thirties after a career break to raise children were regarded as older workers (Metcalfe 1990). Another survey concluded that 'the disadvantage incurred in being "too young" or "too old" was found to impact more on women than men, suggesting that in these age ranges at least, being female acted to intensify age prejudice' (Duncan and Loretto 2004).

The Pensions Act 2007 and the Pensions Act 2008 were part of the government's strategy to implement the recommendations contained in the White Paper *Security in retirement: towards a new pensions*

---

26 Labour Market Statistics July 2012, available at www.statistics.gov.uk.

system (DWP 2006). One of the White Paper's objectives was to 'deliver fairer outcomes for women and carers'. That fairer outcomes are needed for existing and future women recipients of pensions is clear. The White Paper listed the reasons why women generally received lower pensions than men. First, until 1978 the system did not recognise caring responsibilities, with the result that absences from the workforce for such reasons led to periods without contributions, which resulted in a lesser likelihood of reaching the required 39 years' contributions for a full basic state pension. Second, again prior to 1978, women were able to pay a reduced rate of national insurance contribution and rely upon their husband's contributions, thus not having a personal entitlement to a state pension. Third, around 70 per cent of the female pensioner population has no private pension at all. This is because of a lower level of participation in the labour force and the receipt, on average, of lower rates of pay and shorter working hours, as most part-time workers are women. Also, as a result of a longer life expectancy, retired women's savings were required to last longer and investments to produce an annuity resulted in less income than that received by men. It has been calculated that the majority of annuities taken out are done so on a single life basis, so the surviving wife has little or no continuing benefit. Finally, an absence from the labour market has a significant effect on pay levels. On average, women experience a drop in pay of around 16 per cent after a year out of the labour market, which is double that faced by men. The result of these disadvantages is that only 30 per cent of women reaching state pension age are entitled to a full basic state pension, compared with 85 per cent of men (Sargeant 2009b).

9.7 Equality of terms

Part 5, Chapter 3 of the Equality Act 2010 contains provisions aimed at achieving equality between men and women in pay and other terms of employment. There is also a Code of Practice on Equal Pay (EHRC 2011b). The Code states that the purpose of the equal pay provisions in the Equality Act 2010 are to ensure that pay and other employment conditions are determined without sex discrimination or bias. Historically, women 'have often been paid less than men for doing the same or equivalent work and this inequality has persisted in some areas'. The full-time gender pay gap has lessened since 1975 (when the Equal Pay Act 1970 took effect), but there still exists a gap of 16 per cent between womens' and mens' pay.

In order to help achieve this reduction in the gender pay gap, a sex equality clause is implied into terms of employment that do not already contain one (section 66(1) Equality Act 2010). The sex equality clause applies to each term of a person's terms of employment so that each will be comparable (section 66(2)(a) Equality Act 2010). It is not enough, therefore, to say that the terms as a whole are equivalent. Each one needs to be considered separately. This applies where a person is employed on work that 'is equal to the work that a comparator of the opposite sex does' (section 164(1) Equality Act 2010).

In these situations any term of the woman's contract, apart from the equality clause, that is less favourable to the woman than to the comparable man should be modified so as to be not less favourable. Similarly if the woman's contract does not contain a term conferring a benefit on her that is contained in the comparable man's contract, then the woman's contract shall be deemed to include the term. Equal pay must, therefore, be calculated not on the basis of the worth of the overall contract in comparison with the man's contract, but on the basis of each individual item taken in isolation. Where the woman is unable to rely on these provisions, because, for example, there is no comparable man, then she will be able to bring a claim of sex discrimination.

An example is given in the Code of Practice on Equal Pay:

> A female sales manager is entitled under her contract of employment to an annual bonus calculated by reference to a specified number of sales. She discovers that a male sales manager

working for the same employer and in the same office receives a higher bonus under his contract for the same number of sales. She would bring her claim under the equality of terms (equal pay) provisions. However, if the female sales manager is not paid a discretionary Christmas bonus that the male manager is paid, she could bring a claim under the sex discrimination at work provisions rather than an equal pay claim because it is not about a contractual term.

An example of this can be found in *St Helens v Brownbill*,[27] where the claimants were female health care assistants and receptionists working for the NHS Trust. During unsocial hours the women received a lower enhanced rate than their male comparators, although the basic hourly rates were higher for the women than the men. This meant that overall they mostly earned more than their male counterparts. This total amount, according to the court, was not the issue. The principle of equal pay required that there should be equality of each contractual term, which was not the case here.

Succeeding in an equal pay claim will entitle the female complainant to receive the same terms as that comparator. This, in itself, may not always seem fair. *Evesham v North Hertfordshire Health Authority*[28] was an appeal against the remedy awarded by an Employment Tribunal as a result of a long-running claim by speech therapists that their work was of equal value to that of a district clinical psychologist. The claimant was a district chief speech therapist with six years' experience in her post. The comparator was a newly appointed clinical psychologist in his first year and near the bottom of the pay scale. It was argued that she should be placed at a point on the incremental scale that reflected her experience. The Court of Appeal turned down her claim because to do this would entitle her to pay in excess of that received by the male comparator, with whom she had established equal value.

According to section 65 of the Equality Act 2010, A's work is equal to B's work if it is:

(a)   like B's work;
(b)   rated as equivalent to B's work; or
(c)   of equal value to B's work.

9.7.1 'Like work'

The concept of 'like work' focuses on the job rather than the person performing it. It is enough for a person to have shown that his or her work is of the same or broadly similar nature as that of a person of the opposite sex, unless the employer can prove that any differences are not related to sex and are a proportionate means of achieving a legitimate aim (section 69).

According to section 65(2) of the Equality Act 2010, A's work is like B's work if the work is broadly similar and any differences that exist 'are not of practical importance in relation to their terms of work'. Thus in comparing work, a broad approach should be taken and attention must be paid to the frequency with which any differences occur in practice as well as their nature and extent. Trivial differences or 'differences not likely in the real world to be reflected in terms and conditions of employment' are unlikely to be taken into account. In *Capper Pass*[29] the court stated that the issue should be approached in two stages. First, whether the work that is done by the woman and the man is the same or broadly similar and, second, are the differences in what they each do of practical importance in relation to their terms and conditions of employment; for example, would it put them into different grades if there a job evaluation scheme was applied?[30]

---

27 *St Helens & Knowsley Hospitals Trust v Brownbill* [2011] IRLR 815. The court applied a previous House of Lords judgement in *Hayward v Cammell Laird Shipbuilders Ltd* [1988] IRLR 257.
28 [2000] IRLR 257.
29 See *Capper Pass Ltd v Lawton* [1976] IRLR 366.
30 *British Leyland v Powell* [1978] IRLR 57.

Tribunals are required to investigate the actual work done rather than rely on theoretical contractual obligations. The performance of supervisory duties may constitute 'things done' of practical importance,[31] but the time at which the work is done would seem to be irrelevant. In *Dugdale v Kraft Foods*[32] the men and women were employed on broadly similar work, but only men worked the night shift. It was held that the hours at which the work was performed did not prevent equal basic rates being afforded because the men could be compensated for the night shift by an additional payment. Thus an equality clause will not result in equal pay if persons of one sex are remunerated for something that persons of the other sex do not do.[33]

The Code of Practice on Equal Pay gives a good example of the importance of practical differences between the woman's work and that of the male comparator:

> A woman working as a primary school administrator claimed equal pay with a male secondary school administrator. The courts found they were not doing like work. Although the work was broadly similar, the latter role carried greater financial and managerial responsibilities and was in a much larger school. The primary school administrator had more routine, term-time tasks while the secondary school administrator's work was year round and more strategic. These differences were considered to be of practical importance so the equal pay for like work claim failed.[34]

9.7.2 Work rated as equivalent

According to section 66(4) of the Equality Act 2010, a person's work will only be regarded as rated as equivalent to that of a person of the opposite sex if it has been given equal value under a properly conducted job evaluation scheme, including the allocation to a grade or scale at the end of the evaluation process. Thus in *Springboard Trust v Robson*[35] it was accepted that the applicant was employed on work rated as equivalent, notwithstanding that the comparator's job scored different points, where the result of converting the points to grades provided for under the evaluation scheme was that the jobs were to be treated as in the same grade.

A valid job evaluation exercise will evaluate the job and not the person performing it, and if evaluation studies are to be relied on, they must be analytical in the sense of dividing a physical or abstract whole into its constituent parts. It is clearly insufficient if benchmark jobs have been evaluated using a system of job evaluation whereas the jobs of the applicant and comparators have not.[36] Employers are not prevented from using physical effort as a criterion if the tasks involved objectively require a certain level of physical strength, so long as the evaluation system as a whole precludes all sex discrimination by taking into account sex-specific criteria (section 65(4)). If the work has been rated as equivalent, a complainant does not have to show that the employees concerned have actually been paid in accordance with the evaluation scheme.[37]

According to the Court of Appeal, where there is one group that contains a significant number, though not a clear majority, of females whose work is evaluated as equal to that of another group who are predominantly male and receive more pay, the presence of a significant number of men in the disadvantaged group should not preclude an employment tribunal from holding that the disparity requires justification.[38]

---

31 See *Eaton v Nuttall* [1977] IRLR 71.
32 [1976] IRLR 368.
33 See *Thomas v NCB* [1987] IRLR 451 and *Calder v Rowntree Mackintosh* [1993] IRLR 212.
34 See *Morgan v Middlesbrough Borough Council* [2005] EWCA Civ 1432.
35 [1992] IRLR 261.
36 See *Bromley v Quick Ltd* [1988] IRLR 249.
37 See *O'Brien v Sim-Chem Ltd* [1980] IRLR 373.
38 *Bailey v Home Office* [2005] IRLR 369.

9.7.3 Equal value

Section 65(6) of the Equality Act 2010 provides that A's work is of equal value to B's work if it is neither like B's work or rated as equivalent to B's work but is nevertheless equal to B's work in terms of the demands made on A by reference to factors such as effort, skill and decision making.

9.7.4 The comparator

In equal pay comparisons the selection of the comparator is of vital importance. Section 69 of the Equality Act 2010 provides that if A is employed, B is a comparator if either:

(a)   B is employed by A's employer or by an associate of A's employer; and
(b)   A and B work at the same establishment.

or

(a)   B is employed by A's employer or by an associate of A's employer;
(b)   B works at an establishment other than the one at which A works; and
(c)   common terms apply at the establishments (either generally or as between A and B).

So it is not necessary for the two employees to be working at the same establishment, as long as there are common terms of employment between their two establishments. Nor do they have to work for the same employer as they can work for associate employers. Associate means where one company has control of the other of both companies are controlled by a third party (section 79(9)).

9.7.5 Defence of material factor

As has already been stated an employer does have a defence against an apparent breach of a sex equality clause if the employer can show that the material factor upon which he or she is relying, which puts one sex at a disadvantage when compared to the other, is not due to sex and if the factor is a proportionate means of achieving a legitimate aim (section 69(1)–(2) Equality Act 2010). Interestingly, section 69(3) states that the long-term aim of reducing inequality between men and women's terms of work is always to be seen as a legitimate aim.

An example used in the guidance is:

> A firm of accountants structures employees' pay on the basis of success in building relationships with clients (including after hours client functions). Because of domestic responsibilities, fewer women than men can maintain regular client contact and women's pay is much lower. The employer is unable to show the way it rewards client relationship building is proportionate, taking into account the disadvantage to women employees.

Glasgow City Council v Marshall[39] concerned an equal pay claim between instructors and teachers in certain specialist schools. A number of female instructors claimed that they were employed on like work with male teachers and a male instructor claimed that he was employed on like work with a female teacher. After a long hearing, over some 52 days, the instructors won their case at an employment tribunal. The employers appealed against the tribunal's decision on their defence under section 1(3) of the Equal Pay Act (EPA) 1970. Their case was based upon the fact that the sets of

---

39 [2000] IRLR 272.

employees had their terms and agreements settled by different collective bargaining structures. The employers also, with the help of statistics, sought to show an absence of sex discrimination. This latter argument was not appealed against. It was this presumed lack of sex discrimination that undermined the instructors' case, however. The House of Lords held that to exclude matters of sex discrimination would mean that the EPA 1970 was concerned with one employee being paid less than another, rather than with arguments about whether a female employee was paid less than a male comparator. Lord Nicholls stated:

> The scheme of the Act is that a rebuttable presumption of sex discrimination arises once the gender based comparison shows that a woman, doing like work or work rated as equivalent or work of equal value to that of a man, is being paid or treated less favourably than the man.

The burden of proof, according to the House, then passes to the employer who needs to show that the reason for the differences is not tainted with sex.

9.8 Women on boards

We have already made reference to this subject in Chapter 1, but because it is a sex discrimination issue, it is considered further here. There are significant barriers to women progressing at work. One Eurofound report (Eurofound 2009) summed up the situation by stating that:

> Women are underrepresented in managerial jobs compared to their share of overall employment. Also, when climbing up an organisation's hierarchy, the proportion of women managers diminishes sharply. Billing and Alvesson (2000, p. 145)[52] specify that women are outnumbered by men in positions of formal power and authority, high status and high incomes. They state that men have a near monopoly on the most senior positions and they are overrepresented in middle-level managerial jobs globally.

52 Billing, Y.D. and Alvesson, M., 'Questioning the notion of feminine leadership: A critical perspective on the gender labelling of leadership', *Gender, Work and Organization*, Vol. 7, No. 3, 2000, pp. 144–57.

The data for this report came from the Fourth European Working Conditions Survey 2005. This revealed that, in Europe, some 33 per cent of managers were female, but that there were large variations between different countries. The figures were highest in Latvia (51 per cent of managers being female) and most of the Eastern European countries where the rate was over 40 per cent. The lowest rates were in Southern Europe with figures approaching 17 per cent of managers being women, and only 16 per cent in Malta. There is also significant gender segregation with women managers being over-represented in the health and education sectors and being sparse in traditional manufacturing-type enterprises. The big gap develops during the 30 to 49 year age group when the traditional caring roles of women seem to limit their prospects of advancement.

One survey reported on the reasons why there are such a limited number of women on boards of big companies (BIS 2011). Attitude was referred to by some 30 per cent of respondents, with bias, prejudice or stereotypical behaviour being the main factor. A second reason centred on the work environment was also mentioned by 30 per cent of respondents. Other reasons given were career advancement, with too few opportunities for advancement or professional development, or just a lack of encouragement and support. The final main reason concerned recruitment, including the likelihood of men recruiting men and people in their own image.

In 2012 the European Commission proposed a quota system for board membership for listed companies to be 40 per cent female by 2020. Some countries had already implemented or proposed such a system. These countries include Norway, Spain, Iceland, Finland and France.

In France the legislation adopted applied a quota of 40 per cent of directors being female by 2016. At the time of writing this book it is difficult to say whether the EC proposal will be adopted, as some Member States were opposed to the EU taking action on this, believing that it should be left to the Member State to decide. The European Parliament was said to be in favour of the initiative.

The question of imposing quotas in order to achieve any sort of equality is a controversial one. It is a piece of positive discrimination in favour of one group at the expense of another. With respect to the proportion of women on the boards of big companies, it has been estimated that, at the current rate of change, gender parity will not be achieved for another 70 years. It is therefore much more attractive to have a quota policy that will achieve some sort of parity within 10 years or so. On the other hand a quota system is achieved only by discriminating against men and it does seem strange that a policy aimed at overcoming discrimination should achieve its ends by having a policy of discrimination.

9.9 Gender pay gap information and discussions about pay

There are two further measures aimed at helping to reduce the gap in terms of employment between men and women. These are, first, to persuade employers to publish information and protect the exchange of information between employees. Section 78 of the Equality Act 2010 enables the Minister to make regulations requiring employers with at least 250 employees to publish information about the differences in pay between their male and female employees. Initially, though, the government is intent on encouraging employers to do this on a voluntary basis and the Equality and Human Rights Commission is monitoring progress.[40]

Second, section 77(1) of the Equality Act 2010 states:

> A term of a person's work that purports to prevent or restrict the person (P) from disclosing or seeking to disclose information about the terms of P's work is unenforceable against P in so far as P makes or seeks to make a relevant pay disclosure.

A relevant pay disclosure is a disclosure made for the purpose of enabling the person who makes it, or seeks it, to discover if there is a connection between pay and having, or not having, a protected characteristic. Thus such a clause would be unenforceable if the purpose were to find out about the relationship between a woman's pay and that of a man. The Equality and Human Rights Commission offers this example:[41]

> Mr A is a chemist employed by a pharmaceutical company. His contract of employment forbids him discussing his salary either with colleagues or with people from outside of the company. Mr A is thinking about going to work for a rival company and when he meets the rival company's HR Director at the golf club, he asks about possible opportunities and tells the HR Director what he is currently earning. Their conversation is overheard by one of Mr A's colleagues, who mentions it to the Managing Director. The Managing Director takes disciplinary action against Mr A for having breached a clause in his contract of employment. Mr A cannot claim victimisation because he was not making a 'relevant pay disclosure'.

---

40 See http://www.equalityhumanrights.com/advice-and-guidance/guidance-for-employers-pre-october-10/voluntary-gender-pay-gap-reporting/ (last accessed 17 January 2013).
41 See http://www.equalityhumanrights.com/advice-and-guidance/tools-equal-pay/discussing-pay-with-colleagues/protected-discussions-with-colleagues-and-others-about-pay/ (last accessed 17 January 2013).

Mr B works in the City. His contract of employment stipulates that disclosing his salary to colleagues amounts to a disciplinary offence. Mr B tells a female colleague, Ms C, about the size of the bonus he is expecting because she asks him for the information in relation to her own pay negotiations. A few weeks later when the bonuses have been paid, Ms C files a claim for equal pay against their employer. The employer dismisses Mr B for having told Ms C about his bonus payment in breach of the pay secrecy clause in his contract. Because this was a 'relevant pay disclosure' it was a protected act and so Mr B can claim victimisation.

Thus it is not a power to discuss earnings generally, but only in relation to a protected characteristic.

9.10 Summary

This chapter has considered evidence that discrimination against women continues both in terms of sex discrimination and equal pay and how at least formal equality is to be achieved. Some propose that quotas in respect of senior managers within organisations is the answer, but this is to accept that action to correct a wrong can only be achieved by another wrong, that is discrimination against suitable male candidates. It is a difficult balance to be struck and maybe the answer depends upon how long we are prepared to wait for equality and, indeed, whether we think it is likely to happen without even more positive action.

Older women are a particular issue because they continue to suffer disadvantage. They have tended to have a shorter working life punctuated by career breaks and with lower earnings than men. The result has been poverty in old age for many, faced with lower pensions (or none) and the prospect of living longer than men on this income. The Pensions Acts went some way to help by reducing the qualifying years to entitlement to a state pension to 20, but this only applied to future retirees, leaving a whole generation of women with a life of lower incomes resulting from them carrying out traditional women's roles.

Chapter 10

Sexual Orientation and Gender Reassignment

Chapter Contents

10.1 Introduction

Sexual orientation and gender reassignment are two of the protected characteristics listed in section 4 of the Equality Act 2010. They are, of course, linked in the sense that they are both characteristics of expressing ones true sexual identity, but they are also different enough to justify separate consideration in this chapter. Because of their common interests they are often put together in one acronym – LGBT, meaning lesbians, gay men, bisexuals and transgender people.

10.2 Sexual orientation

Section 12 of the Equality Act 2010 provides that sexual orientation means sexual orientation towards:

(a)   persons of the same sex;
(b)   persons of the opposite sex; or
(c)   persons of either sex.

Thus the legislation protects gay men and lesbians, who are attracted to people of their own sex, heterosexuals who are attracted to the opposite sex and bisexuals who experience attraction to both men and women.

There is a fourth group who may or may not be included in this protection, namely asexuals. It has been estimated that about one per cent of the population is asexual, that is not attracted to any other sex.[1] One researcher, Professor Anthony Bogaert, defines asexuality as an enduring, complete lack of sexual attraction. He says that there are two types: 'people who have some level of sex drive, but don't direct this drive toward others, and other people who have no sex drive whatsoever' (Bogaert 2012). It is not clear whether this group would be protected by the legislation, especially as most are likely to be single people. Single people, unlike those who are married or in a civil partnership, are not a category protected by the Equality Act 2010.

10.3 LGBT

The Equality Act makes unlawful direct and indirect discrimination, harassment and victimisation in relation to sexual orientation. In HM Land Registry v Grant[2] a man who was a homosexual complained about a number of incidents that he claimed amounted to discrimination and harassment on the grounds of his sexuality. The EAT commented on the fact that he had chosen to reveal his sexuality and that the position would have been different if he had not 'come out'. Then a remark about his sexuality might have had a much more devastating impact. Another harassment situation occurred in English v Thomas Sanderson Blinds Ltd,[3] where a man who was not a homosexual was nevertheless subjected to a campaign of harassment on the basis that he was and which occurred despite those who took part in the harassment knowing that he was not homosexual. This was still held to be harassment within the definition of the regulations making such actions unlawful.

---

1 See http://english.cntv.cn/20120822/103035.shtml (last accessed 17 January 2013).
2 HM Land Registry v Grant [2010] IRLR 583.
3 [2009] IRLR 206.

There are large numbers of people who are LGBT. The statistics are estimates because of the perceived difficulty in asking people about their sexual orientation/gender identity. It is estimated that in the UK some 5–7 per cent of the population is LGBT. This results in a figure of up to some four million people. Projections of growth in the older population also suggest that, by 2031, there will be 1 million to 1.4 million people over the age of 60 who are lesbian, gay or bisexual. All the figures are, however, only estimates with various surveys giving a range of from 0.3 per cent to 7 per cent of the population (Mitchell et al. 2009).

Bisexuals are people attracted to both sexes and, therefore, cannot be defined in the same way as lesbians and gay men. The 2002 US National Survey of Family Growth found that nearly 13 per cent of women and 6 per cent of men were attracted to both men and women; 2 per cent identified themselves as bisexual, compared to 1.8 per cent who identified themselves as homosexual (Miller et al. 2007). Other studies have estimated the numbers of bisexuals from between 2 per cent and 15 per cent of the population. In each study the incidence of bisexuality was greater than that of homosexuality.

10.3.1 Discrimination

The history of society's attitudes to homosexuality in recent generations has not been an attractive one and understanding of it is a recent phenomenon. An older gay man or lesbian today would have likely lived through some difficult times. In the 1930s homosexuality was regarded as a psychiatric disorder that required therapeutic intervention. Methods of treatment included drugs, aversion therapy, lobotomies and electric shock treatment (Knauer 2009). It was not until 1967 that the Sexual Offences Act was adopted in the UK. This provided that homosexual acts in private did not constitute an offence, provided that it was consensual and that the participants were over 21 years of age.[4] It was not until 1973 that the American Psychiatric Association removed homosexuality from its list of mental disorders and it was only in 1992 that the World Health Organisation declassified homosexuality as a mental illness. It was from 2003 onwards that the UK started to make discrimination against people on the grounds of their sexual orientation unlawful with the adoption of the Equal Opportunities in Employment (Sexual Orientation) Regulations,[5] and it was not until 2007 that this became unlawful in respect of facilities, goods and services (the Equality Act (Sexual Orientation) Regulations).[6]

In contrast, in many parts of the USA it is still not unlawful to discriminate against LGBT people. The situation is probably worse for transgender people than for lesbians and gay men. A San Francisco report (San Francisco Human Rights Commission 2003) summed up the situation:

> The older population of the Lesbian Gay Bisexual Transgender (LGBT) communities, particularly those over 60, have lived for decades in a society where LGBT people have been scorned, discriminated against, disowned by their families and religious institutions, fired from their jobs, arrested, beaten, and murdered. Though these conditions are vastly improved in today's San Francisco, all of these things still happen to some degree. Older LGBT people have learned to survive under these hostile conditions by staying in the closet or otherwise 'keeping a low profile'.

In 1969 people fought back against police harassment at the now famous Stonewall Inn in Greenwich Village, New York. In June of that year:

---

4 Section 1(1) Sexual Offences Act 1967.
5 SI 2003/1661.
6 Both now superseded by the Equality Act 2010.

the New York City police department went on a routine assignment to harass patrons and to close a gay bar in Greenwich Village. They were unexpectedly faced with the anger and indignation of a handful of men and women who felt that they had had enough. That night began subsequent rioting and brought gays out of their 'closet' around the city. This capped a history of quietly suffered oppression (Kochman 1997).

Three years earlier at the Compton Street Café in the Tenderloin district of San Francisco there was a similar event when transgender people resisted police harassment and fought back.

Despite all that has gone before, there are still significant levels of discrimination present. For example, one UK sponsored study (Ellinson and Gunstone 2009) found that:

> When asked about incidents of prejudice and discrimination that were related to their sexual orientation, the majority of gay men (63 per cent) and lesbians (66 per cent) said they had experienced name calling and other forms of verbal abuse. Around half of lesbians and gay men and a third of bisexual men and women reported that they had suffered stress. Around four in ten lesbians and gay men reported that they had been bullied, or felt frightened, and had suffered from low self-esteem. Around one in five gay men reported that they had been physically assaulted and six per cent of lesbians that they had been sexually assaulted. Nine per cent of gay men and fourteen per cent of bisexual men reported a current mental health condition, as did 16 per cent of lesbians and over a quarter (26 per cent) of bisexual women. This contrasts sharply with just 3 per cent of heterosexual men and eight per cent of heterosexual women.

Whilst homophobia results in a dislike of LGBT people, heterosexism results from a belief that homosexuality is inferior to heterosexuality. Institutional heterosexism, it is suggested, results from a social, economic and legal system that disparages homosexuality (Mitchell et al. 2009). An example of this can be found in health care and the treatment of older LGBT people. When support is needed, a person's vulnerability to discrimination might be increased. One example of this cited in research is the gay man caring for his dying partner who receives little support from neighbours and has a doctor who asks him if his wife has died (Ward et al. 2008). In a further US study of some 205 older LGBTs, it was said that their greatest fear about growing older was being or dying alone. Some 19 per cent also stated that they had little or no confidence that medical personnel would treat them with dignity and respect as LGBT people (MetLife Mature Market Institute 2006). A UK study (River 2006) stated, in respect of care homes, that:

> The older lesbians we talked to said they would be worried how other residents would react. Older lesbians responded with comments such as 'it would be a nightmare' and 'I am hoping never to need one'. The perceptions behind these latter comments are, of course, shared by most heterosexual older people. However, older lesbians have particular concerns over and above the basic fears (amplified by television publicity about appallingly bad practice in some homes).

10.4 Gender reassignment

Gender reassignment is a protected characteristic. According to section 7 of the Equality Act 2010 a person has this protected characteristic if the person is proposing to undergo, is undergoing or has undergone a process (or part of a process) for the purpose of reassigning the person's sex by changing physiological or other attributes of sex. A man transitioning to being a woman and a woman transitioning to being a man both share the characteristic of gender reassignment.

Section 7(2) provides that all transsexual people are included. These provisions are similar to those previously in the Sex Discrimination Act (SDA) 1975, except that there is no longer a need for the person to be under medical supervision in order to come within the definition. According to the Statutory Code of Practice on Employment (EHRC 2011a), 'gender reassignment' is a personal process, that is moving away from one's birth sex to the preferred gender, rather than a medical process. There is no requirement for a person to undergo any medical process in order to receive protection. It is enough that the gender reassignment is proposed, but there is no requirement to go further. The Code of Practice gives this example:

> A person who was born physically male decides to spend the rest of his life living as a woman. He declares his intention to his manager at work, who makes appropriate arrangements, and she then starts life at work and at home as a woman. She eventually decides to start hormone treatment and starts hormone treatment; after several years she goes through gender reassignment surgery. Throughout this process she would have the protected characteristic of gender reassignment for the purposes of the Act.

Section 16 of the Equality Act 2010 provides that less favourable treatment in relation to absences from work, because of sickness, injury or some other reason connected to the person proposing or undergoing (or having undergone) the gender reassignment process, also amounts to discrimination on the protected characteristic of gender reassignment. The Code of Practice on Employment also states that there is no requirement for an individual to inform their employer of their gender reassignment status, but that they may want to discuss it with their employer if they are proposing to go through with it, in order to obtain the support of the employer.

Transgender is a generic term applied to trans people and can be described as follows:

> A very broad term to include all sorts of trans people. It includes cross dressers, people who wear a mix of clothing, people with a dual or no gender identity, and transsexual people. It is also used to define a political and social community which is inclusive of transsexual people, transgender people, cross-dressers (transvestites) and other groups of 'gender-variant' people (Whittle et al. 2007).

Quite apart from the discrimination suffered as a result of their eventual sexual orientation, transgender people may go through a process of being exposed to bigotry and prejudice whilst undergoing serious physical and mental life-changing processes. It is the public nature of transgenderism that is an issue both for the individuals and for their supporters and friends. It is often the partners who are in the front line. Heterosexual partners can find themselves perceived as lesbian or gay when their partner has changed to the same sex.

Gender dysphoria is a condition where people feel that they are trapped in a body of the wrong sex and a transsexual is someone with an extreme and long-term case of gender dysphoria, who seeks to alter their biological sex to match their gender identity. Gender dysphoria can also be known as gender identity disorder, gender incongruence or transgenderism.[7] It is estimated that there are some 4,000 people in the UK who are receiving medical help for gender dysphoria, indicating a total of some 15,000 in all. This cannot, of course, be an accurate measure of the number of transgender people, but it does suggest that they constitute a substantial

---

7 See http://www.nhs.uk/conditions/gender-dysphoria/Pages/Introduction.aspx?url=Pages/What-is-it.aspx (last accessed 17 January 2013).

number.[8] Studies carried out in the Netherlands suggest that the prevalence of transsexualism is between 1:11,900 and 1:17,000 in men over 15 years of age. The number of female-to-male transsexual people is far smaller, possibly in the region of one to every five male-to-female transsexual people. A further study carried out in primary care units in Scotland estimated the prevalence in men over 15 years at 1:12,400, with an approximate sex ratio of one to four in favour of male-to-female patients. These studies suggest that in the UK there are between 1,300 and 2,000 male-to-female and between 250 and 400 female-to-male transsexual people. The report 'Press for Change', however, estimates the figures at around 5,000 post-operative transsexual people (Home Office 2000).

Prior to the Equality Act 2010, gender reassignment was treated as a sex discrimination issue. *P v S and Cornwall County Council*,[9] for example, concerned an employee who informed their employer of an intention to undergo gender reassignment. The first part of this was to undertake a 'life test', which consisted of spending a year living in the manner of the proposed gender. Whilst on sick leave for initial surgery, the employee was dismissed. The Employment Tribunal decided that the individual had been dismissed because of the gender reassignment, but decided that the SDA 1975 did not apply to these circumstances. They referred the matter to the ECJ with the question as to whether the Equal Treatment Directive provided for this situation. The ECJ held that the Directive sought to safeguard the principle of equality and applied, although not exclusively, to discrimination on the grounds of sex. The Court held that discrimination on the basis of gender reassignment was to treat a person less favourably than persons of the sex to which the individual had been deemed to belong before the gender reassignment and was therefore contrary to Article 5(1) of the Equal Treatment Directive.

Another pre-Equality Act 2010 example of discrimination on this ground was in *Chessington World of Adventures Ltd v Reed*,[10] where an individual announced a change of gender from male to female and, as a result, was subjected to continuous harassment from her work colleagues. She was eventually absent through sickness and then dismissed. The EAT confirmed the Employment Tribunal's view that the employer, who had known of the harassment, was directly liable for the sex discrimination that had taken place.

The Gender Recognition Act 2004 provides that a person over the age of 18 years may make an application for a gender recognition certificate. The application will be reviewed by a Gender Recognition Panel, who will grant a certificate if certain conditions are met. These are that the applicant has or has had gender dysphoria, has lived in the acquired gender throughout the period of two years ending with the date on which the application is made and intends to continue to live in the acquired gender until death. The other condition is that the person changing gender is not married or in a civil partnership, as same sex marriages or opposite sex civil partnerships are not permitted. Whilst one can see the logic of this, it does seem to add a potentially painful issue on top of all the other difficult issues being dealt with. The effect of obtaining a gender recognition certificate is to acquire legal status for the sought-for gender. The Code of Practice on Employment states[11] that transsexual people should not be routinely asked to produce their gender recognition certificate to prove their legal gender as this would compromise the person's right to privacy. If the employer requires proof of a person's legal gender, then their new birth certificate should be treated as sufficient.

---

8 See the NHS website at http://www.nhs.uk/conditions/gender-dysphoria/Pages/Introduction.aspx?url=Pages/What-is-it.aspx (last accessed 17 January 2013). This National Health Service website also reveals that men are diagnosed with gender dysphoria five times more often than women.

9 Case 13/94 *P v S and Cornwall County Council* [1996] IRLR 347 ECJ.

10 [1997] IRLR 556.

11 Para 2.30.

10.5 Marriage or civil partnership

Section 8 of the Equality Act 2010 makes marriage or civil partnership a protected characteristic and section 13(4) ensures that it is only people who are married or in a civil partnership who are protected. Single people are not protected, nor are those who intend to get married or enter a civil partnership. Those who have divorced or had their civil partnership dissolved are not protected either.

The Equality Act 2010 also provides that discrimination by association is not included for this protected characteristic. In addition direct discrimination only covers less favourable treatment of a worker because the worker is in fact married or a civil partner.[12] The issues related to marriage between heterosexual couples are considered in Chapter 9 on sex discrimination. Here we only consider this issue in relation to same sex couples.

The possibility of having a civil partnership was created in December 2005 when the Civil Partnership Act 2004 came into effect. Section 1 of this Act provides that civil partnerships are between same sex couples. It gives same sex couples the right to form legally recognised relationships that give the participants similar rights as heterosexual couples who get married. A major difference between the two events (marriage and civil partnership) is that civil partnership ceremonies are not allowed to contain any religious element. Issues concerned with civil partnerships are also likely to be issues concerned with discrimination in connection with the protected characteristic of sexual orientation. The extent to which this has caused problems for those who are members of religions or belief systems that do not approve of homosexuality or same sex marriages are discussed in Chapter 8 on religion or belief.

In 2012 the Government Equalities Office issued a consultation (Government Equalities Office 2012) on the possibility of introducing same sex marriages rather than just having civil partnerships. Despite a civil partnership giving its participants the same rights as those in a heterosexual marriage, there is still a demand for same sex relationships to be put on a par with heterosexual marriages. According to the consultation, 'it was argued by some that having two separate provisions for same-sex and opposite-sex couples perpetuates misconceptions and discrimination'. The document made the government's intention quite clear:

> We recognise that the personal commitment made by same-sex couples when they enter into a civil partnership is no different to the commitment made by opposite-sex couples when they enter into a marriage. We do not think that the ban on same-sex couples getting married should continue. Put simply, it's not right that a couple who love each other and want to formalise a commitment to each other should be denied the right to marry.

The essential difference between a marriage and a civil partnership is that a marriage can be either a religious event or a civil affair; a civil partnership can only be a civil event and religion is excluded. The government's proposals were limited in that they did not intend to permit same sex marriages on religious premises, but to ensure that same sex marriages could take place but only as civil events.

The government proposed:

(a)   to remove the ban on same sex couples being able to have a marriage through a civil ceremony. The proposal stated that:

---

12 Section 13(4) Equality Act 2010.

> The Government recognises that the commitment made between a man and a man, or a woman and a woman in a civil partnership is as significant as the commitment between a man and a woman in a civil marriage. If we recognise the commitment being made is as significant, it is only right that the Government provides couples with the same opportunity to recognise that commitment in the valued institution of marriage.

(b)   to make no changes to how religious organisations solemnise marriages, meaning that marriages that consist of a religious ceremony and on religious premises would still only be legally possible between a man and a woman.

(c)   to allow transsexual people to change their legal gender without having to legally end their existing marriage or civil partnership (see above). This would be a big step forward as it would enable people to stay together in marriage even though one of the partners had changed gender.

Maruko[13] concerned someone who had entered into a registered civil partnership under German law. His partner had belonged to a pension scheme for many years. When he died Mr Maruko applied to the pension scheme for a widower's pension. This was refused because the pension scheme rules only provided an entitlement for surviving spouses, not partners. The Court of Justice concluded, amongst other matters, that treating life partners differently to surviving spouses in relation to survivor's benefits would amount to less favourable treatment and would therefore be direct discrimination on the grounds of sexual orientation. This is a significant first step by the Court of Justice in establishing the principle of equal treatment with regard to sexual orientation.

10.6 Summary

Protection against discrimination on the grounds of sexual orientation and gender reassignment are recent and much welcome innovations in British law. In many other parts of the world, including much of the USA, it is not unlawful to discriminate against gay men or lesbians because of their sexuality.

The major issue has been, and continues to be, the conflict with the protection offered against discrimination on the grounds of religion or belief (this is dealt with in Chapter 8). Many people hold the view that homosexuality is wrong and the question is whether we should acknowledge this and weaken the legislation on sexual orientation or whether we should lessen the choice of those with a strong religious faith. The Equality Act 2010 does recognise this to a limited extent and permits an exception to the principle of non-discrimination in certain circumstances, but to go beyond this will limit the human rights of gay, lesbian and transgender people.

---

13 C-267/06 *Maruko v Versorgungsanstalt Der Deutschen Bühnen* [2008] IRLR 405.

Appendix

Equality Act 2010 Part 2

EQUALITY: KEY CONCEPTS

CHAPTER 1 PROTECTED CHARACTERISTICS

4 The protected characteristics

The following characteristics are protected characteristics –

age;
disability;
gender reassignment;
marriage and civil partnership;
pregnancy and maternity;
race;
religion or belief;
sex;
sexual orientation.

5 Age

(1) In relation to the protected characteristic of age –

  (a) a reference to a person who has a particular protected characteristic is a reference to a person of a particular age group;

  (b) a reference to persons who share a protected characteristic is a reference to persons of the same age group.

(2) A reference to an age group is a reference to a group of persons defined by reference to age, whether by reference to a particular age or to a range of ages.

6 Disability

(1) A person (P) has a disability if –

  (a) P has a physical or mental impairment, and

  (b) the impairment has a substantial and long-term adverse effect on P's ability to carry out normal day-to-day activities.

(2)   A reference to a disabled person is a reference to a person who has a disability.

(3)   In relation to the protected characteristic of disability –

(a)   a reference to a person who has a particular protected characteristic is a reference to a person who has a particular disability;

(b)   a reference to persons who share a protected characteristic is a reference to persons who have the same disability.

(4)   This Act (except Part 12 and section 190) applies in relation to a person who has had a disability as it applies in relation to a person who has the disability; accordingly (except in that Part and that section) –

(a)   a reference (however expressed) to a person who has a disability includes a reference to a person who has had the disability, and

(b)   a reference (however expressed) to a person who does not have a disability includes a reference to a person who has not had the disability.

(5)   A Minister of the Crown may issue guidance about matters to be taken into account in deciding any question for the purposes of subsection (1).

(6)   Schedule 1 (disability: supplementary provision) has effect.

7 Gender reassignment

(1)   A person has the protected characteristic of gender reassignment if the person is proposing to undergo, is undergoing or has undergone a process (or part of a process) for the purpose of reassigning the person's sex by changing physiological or other attributes of sex.

(2)   A reference to a transsexual person is a reference to a person who has the protected characteristic of gender reassignment.

(3)   In relation to the protected characteristic of gender reassignment –

(a)   a reference to a person who has a particular protected characteristic is a reference to a transsexual person;

(b)   a reference to persons who share a protected characteristic is a reference to transsexual persons.

8 Marriage and civil partnership

(1)   A person has the protected characteristic of marriage and civil partnership if the person is married or is a civil partner.

(2)   In relation to the protected characteristic of marriage and civil partnership –

(a)   a reference to a person who has a particular protected characteristic is a reference to a person who is married or is a civil partner;

(b)   a reference to persons who share a protected characteristic is a reference to persons who are married or are civil partners.

9 Race

(1)   Race includes –

(a)   colour;

(b)   nationality;

(c)   ethnic or national origins.

(2) In relation to the protected characteristic of race –

  (a) a reference to a person who has a particular protected characteristic is a reference to a person of a particular racial group;
  (b) a reference to persons who share a protected characteristic is a reference to persons of the same racial group.

(3) A racial group is a group of persons defined by reference to race; and a reference to a person's racial group is a reference to a racial group into which the person falls.

(4) The fact that a racial group comprises two or more distinct racial groups does not prevent it from constituting a particular racial group.

(5) A Minister of the Crown may by order –

  (a) amend this section so as to provide for caste to be an aspect of race;
  (b) amend this Act so as to provide for an exception to a provision of this Act to apply, or not to apply, to caste or to apply, or not to apply, to caste in specified circumstances.

(6) The power under section 207(4)(b), in its application to subsection (5), includes power to amend this Act.

10 Religion or belief

(1) Religion means any religion and a reference to religion includes a reference to a lack of religion.

(2) Belief means any religious or philosophical belief and a reference to belief includes a reference to a lack of belief.

(3) In relation to the protected characteristic of religion or belief –

  (a) a reference to a person who has a particular protected characteristic is a reference to a person of a particular religion or belief;
  (b) a reference to persons who share a protected characteristic is a reference to persons who are of the same religion or belief.

11 Sex
In relation to the protected characteristic of sex –

(a) a reference to a person who has a particular protected characteristic is a reference to a man or to a woman;
(b) a reference to persons who share a protected characteristic is a reference to persons of the same sex.

12 Sexual orientation

(1) Sexual orientation means a person's sexual orientation towards –

  (a) persons of the same sex,
  (b) persons of the opposite sex, or
  (c) persons of either sex.

(2) In relation to the protected characteristic of sexual orientation –

  (a) a reference to a person who has a particular protected characteristic is a reference to a person who is of a particular sexual orientation;
  (b) a reference to persons who share a protected characteristic is a reference to persons who are of the same sexual orientation.

CHAPTER 2 PROHIBITED CONDUCT

Discrimination

13 Direct discrimination

(1)   A person (A) discriminates against another (B) if, because of a protected characteristic, A treats B less favourably than A treats or would treat others.

(2)   If the protected characteristic is age, A does not discriminate against B if A can show A's treatment of B to be a proportionate means of achieving a legitimate aim.

(3)   If the protected characteristic is disability, and B is not a disabled person, A does not discriminate against B only because A treats or would treat disabled persons more favourably than A treats B.

(4)   If the protected characteristic is marriage and civil partnership, this section applies to a contravention of Part 5 (work) only if the treatment is because it is B who is married or a civil partner.

(5)   If the protected characteristic is race, less favourable treatment includes segregating B from others.

(6)   If the protected characteristic is sex –

   (a)   less favourable treatment of a woman includes less favourable treatment of her because she is breast-feeding;

   (b)   in a case where B is a man, no account is to be taken of special treatment afforded to a woman in connection with pregnancy or childbirth.

(7)   Subsection (6)(a) does not apply for the purposes of Part 5 (work).

(8)   This section is subject to sections 17(6) and 18(7).

14 Combined discrimination: dual characteristics

(1)   A person (A) discriminates against another (B) if, because of a combination of two relevant protected characteristics, A treats B less favourably than A treats or would treat a person who does not share either of those characteristics.

(2)   The relevant protected characteristics are –

   (a)   age;
   (b)   disability;
   (c)   gender reassignment;
   (d)   race;
   (e)   religion or belief;
   (f)   sex;
   (g)   sexual orientation.

(3)   For the purposes of establishing a contravention of this Act by virtue of subsection (1), B need not show that A's treatment of B is direct discrimination because of each of the characteristics in the combination (taken separately).

(4)   But B cannot establish a contravention of this Act by virtue of subsection (1) if, in reliance on another provision of this Act or any other enactment, A shows that A's treatment of B is not direct discrimination because of either or both of the characteristics in the combination.

(5)   Subsection (1) does not apply to a combination of characteristics that includes disability in circumstances where, if a claim of direct discrimination because of disability were to be brought, it would come within section 116 (special educational needs).

(6) A Minister of the Crown may by order amend this section so as to –

    (a) make further provision about circumstances in which B can, or in which B cannot, establish a contravention of this Act by virtue of subsection (1);

    (b) specify other circumstances in which subsection (1) does not apply.

(7) The references to direct discrimination are to a contravention of this Act by virtue of section 13.

15 Discrimination arising from disability

(1) A person (A) discriminates against a disabled person (B) if –

    (a) A treats B unfavourably because of something arising in consequence of B's disability; and

    (b) A cannot show that the treatment is a proportionate means of achieving a legitimate aim.

(2) Subsection (1) does not apply if A shows that A did not know, and could not reasonably have been expected to know, that B had the disability.

16 Gender reassignment discrimination: cases of absence from work

(1) This section has effect for the purposes of the application of Part 5 (work) to the protected characteristic of gender reassignment.

(2) A person (A) discriminates against a transsexual person (B) if, in relation to an absence of B's that is because of gender reassignment, A treats B less favourably than A would treat B if –

    (a) B's absence was because of sickness or injury; or

    (b) B's absence was for some other reason and it is not reasonable for B to be treated less favourably.

(3) A person's absence is because of gender reassignment if it is because the person is proposing to undergo, is undergoing or has undergone the process (or part of the process) mentioned in section 7(1).

17 Pregnancy and maternity discrimination: non-work cases

(1) his section has effect for the purposes of the application to the protected characteristic of pregnancy and maternity of –

    (a) Part 3 (services and public functions);

    (b) Part 4 (premises);

    (c) Part 6 (education);

    (d) Part 7 (associations).

(2) A person (A) discriminates against a woman if A treats her unfavourably because of a pregnancy of hers.

(3) A person (A) discriminates against a woman if, in the period of 26 weeks beginning with the day on which she gives birth, A treats her unfavourably because she has given birth.

(4) The reference in subsection (3) to treating a woman unfavourably because she has given birth includes, in particular, a reference to treating her unfavourably because she is breast-feeding.

(5) For the purposes of this section, the day on which a woman gives birth is the day on which –

    (a) she gives birth to a living child; or

    (b) she gives birth to a dead child (more than 24 weeks of the pregnancy having passed).

(6) Section 13, so far as relating to sex discrimination, does not apply to anything done in relation to a woman in so far as –

    (a) it is for the reason mentioned in subsection (2); or

    (b) it is in the period, and for the reason, mentioned in subsection (3).

18 Pregnancy and maternity discrimination: work cases

(1) This section has effect for the purposes of the application of Part 5 (work) to the protected characteristic of pregnancy and maternity.

(2) A person (A) discriminates against a woman if, in the protected period in relation to a pregnancy of hers, A treats her unfavourably –

    (a) because of the pregnancy; or

    (b) because of illness suffered by her as a result of it.

(3) A person (A) discriminates against a woman if A treats her unfavourably because she is on compulsory maternity leave.

(4) A person (A) discriminates against a woman if A treats her unfavourably because she is exercising or seeking to exercise, or has exercised or sought to exercise, the right to ordinary or additional maternity leave.

(5) For the purposes of subsection (2), if the treatment of a woman is in implementation of a decision taken in the protected period, the treatment is to be regarded as occurring in that period (even if the implementation is not until after the end of that period).

(6) The protected period, in relation to a woman's pregnancy, begins when the pregnancy begins, and ends –

    (a) if she has the right to ordinary and additional maternity leave, at the end of the additional maternity leave period or (if earlier) when she returns to work after the pregnancy;

    (b) if she does not have that right, at the end of the period of 2 weeks beginning with the end of the pregnancy.

(7) Section 13, so far as relating to sex discrimination, does not apply to treatment of a woman in so far as –

    (a) it is in the protected period in relation to her and is for a reason mentioned in paragraph (a) or (b) of subsection (2); or

    (b) it is for a reason mentioned in subsection (3) or (4).

19 Indirect discrimination

(1) A person (A) discriminates against another (B) if A applies to B a provision, criterion or practice which is discriminatory in relation to a relevant protected characteristic of B's.

(2) For the purposes of subsection (1), a provision, criterion or practice is discriminatory in relation to a relevant protected characteristic of B's if –

(a)   A applies, or would apply, it to persons with whom B does not share the characteristic,

(b)   it puts, or would put, persons with whom B shares the characteristic at a particular disadvantage when compared with persons with whom B does not share it,

(c)   it puts, or would put, B at that disadvantage, and

(d)   A cannot show it to be a proportionate means of achieving a legitimate aim.

(3)   The relevant protected characteristics are –

age;
disability;
gender reassignment;
marriage and civil partnership;
race;
religion or belief;
sex;
sexual orientation.

Adjustments for disabled persons

20 Duty to make adjustments

(1)   Where this Act imposes a duty to make reasonable adjustments on a person, this section, sections 21 and 22 and the applicable Schedule apply; and for those purposes, a person on whom the duty is imposed is referred to as A.

(2)   The duty comprises the following three requirements.

(3)   The first requirement is a requirement, where a provision, criterion or practice of A's puts a disabled person at a substantial disadvantage in relation to a relevant matter in comparison with persons who are not disabled, to take such steps as it is reasonable to have to take to avoid the disadvantage.

(4)   The second requirement is a requirement, where a physical feature puts a disabled person at a substantial disadvantage in relation to a relevant matter in comparison with persons who are not disabled, to take such steps as it is reasonable to have to take to avoid the disadvantage.

(5)   The third requirement is a requirement, where a disabled person would, but for the provision of an auxiliary aid, be put at a substantial disadvantage in relation to a relevant matter in comparison with persons who are not disabled, to take such steps as it is reasonable to have to take to provide the auxiliary aid.

(6)   Where the first or third requirement relates to the provision of information, the steps which it is reasonable for A to have to take include steps for ensuring that in the circumstances concerned the information is provided in an accessible format.

(7)   A person (A) who is subject to a duty to make reasonable adjustments is not (subject to express provision to the contrary) entitled to require a disabled person, in relation to whom A is required to comply with the duty, to pay to any extent A's costs of complying with the duty.

(8)   A reference in section 21 or 22 or an applicable Schedule to the first, second or third requirement is to be construed in accordance with this section.

(9)   In relation to the second requirement, a reference in this section or an applicable Schedule to avoiding a substantial disadvantage includes a reference to –

(a)   removing the physical feature in question;

(b)   altering it; or

(c)   providing a reasonable means of avoiding it.

(10) A reference in this section, section 21 or 22 or an applicable Schedule (apart from paragraphs 2 to 4 of Schedule 4) to a physical feature is a reference to –

(a) a feature arising from the design or construction of a building;

(b) a feature of an approach to, exit from or access to a building;

(c) a fixture or fitting, or furniture, furnishings, materials, equipment or other chattels, in or on premises; or

(d) any other physical element or quality.

(11) A reference in this section, sections 21 or 22 or an applicable Schedule to an auxiliary aid includes a reference to an auxiliary service.

(12) A reference in this section or an applicable Schedule to chattels is to be read, in relation to Scotland, as a reference to moveable property.

21 Failure to comply with duty

(1) A failure to comply with the first, second or third requirement is a failure to comply with a duty to make reasonable adjustments.

(2) A discriminates against a disabled person if A fails to comply with that duty in relation to that person.

(3) A provision of an applicable Schedule which imposes a duty to comply with the first, second or third requirement applies only for the purpose of establishing whether A has contravened this Act by virtue of subsection (2); a failure to comply is, accordingly, not actionable by virtue of another provision of this Act or otherwise.

22 Excluded

23 Comparison by reference to circumstances

(1) On a comparison of cases for the purposes of sections 13, 14, or 19 there must be no material difference between the circumstances relating to each case.

(2) The circumstances relating to a case include a person's abilities if –

(a) on a comparison for the purposes of section 13, the protected characteristic is disability;

(b) on a comparison for the purposes of section 14, one of the protected characteristics in the combination is disability.

(3) If the protected characteristic is sexual orientation, the fact that one person (whether or not the person referred to as B) is a civil partner while another is married is not a material difference between the circumstances relating to each case.

24 Irrelevance of alleged discriminator's characteristics

(1) For the purpose of establishing a contravention of this Act by virtue of section 13(1), it does not matter whether A has the protected characteristic.

(2) For the purpose of establishing a contravention of this Act by virtue of section 14(1), it does not matter –

(a) whether A has one of the protected characteristics in the combination;

(b) whether A has both.

25 Excluded

Other prohibited conduct

26 Harassment

(1)   A person (A) harasses another (B) if –

   (a)   A engages in unwanted conduct related to a relevant protected characteristic, and
   (b)   the conduct has the purpose or effect of –

      (i)   violating B's dignity; or
      (ii)   creating an intimidating, hostile, degrading, humiliating or offensive environment for B.

(2)   A also harasses B if –

   (a)   A engages in unwanted conduct of a sexual nature; and
   (b)   the conduct has the purpose or effect referred to in subsection (1)(b).

(3)   A also harasses B if –

   (a)   A or another person engages in unwanted conduct of a sexual nature or that is related to gender reassignment or sex;
   (b)   the conduct has the purpose or effect referred to in subsection (1)(b); and
   (c)   because of B's rejection of or submission to the conduct, A treats B less favourably than A would treat B if B had not rejected or submitted to the conduct.

(4)   In deciding whether conduct has the effect referred to in subsection (1)(b), each of the following must be taken into account –

   (a)   the perception of B;
   (b)   the other circumstances of the case;
   (c)   whether it is reasonable for the conduct to have that effect.

(5)   The relevant protected characteristics are –

age;
disability;
gender reassignment;
race;
religion or belief;
sex;
sexual orientation.

27 Victimisation

(1)   A person (A) victimises another person (B) if A subjects B to a detriment because –

   (a)   B does a protected act; or
   (b)   A believes that B has done, or may do, a protected act.

(2)   Each of the following is a protected act –

   (a)   bringing proceedings under this Act;
   (b)   giving evidence or information in connection with proceedings under this Act;

(c)   doing any other thing for the purposes of or in connection with this Act;

(d)   making an allegation (whether or not express) that A or another person has contravened this Act.

(3)   Giving false evidence or information, or making a false allegation, is not a protected act if the evidence or information is given, or the allegation is made, in bad faith.

(4)   This section applies only where the person subjected to a detriment is an individual.

(5)   The reference to contravening this Act includes a reference to committing a breach of an equality clause or rule.

Bibliography

Age Reference Group on Human Rights Age Concern England (2005) *Age and ... Multiple Discrimination and Older People*, available at: http://www.ageuk.org.uk/Documents/en-GB/For-professionals/Research/Age%20and%20Multiple%20Discrimination%20(2005)_pro.pdf?dtrk=true.

BIS (2011) *Women on Boards*, available at: http://www.bis.gov.uk/assets/biscore/business-law/docs/w/11-745-women-on-boards.pdf.

Bogaert, A. (2012) *Understanding Asexuality*. Lanham: Rowman & Littlefield Publishers.

Bond, S., Hollywood, E. and Colgan, F. (2009) *Integration in the Workplace: Emerging Employment Practice; on Age, Sexual Orientation and Religion or Belief*. Manchester: Equality and Human Rights Commission.

Butler, R.N. (1969) 'Age-ism: another form of bigotry' *Gerontologist* 9, 243–46.

Capital Economics London (2007) 'Net Migration has peaked', January, available at: www.capitaleconomics.com.

Citizens' Advice Bureau (2007), *Rooting Out the Rogues*, available at: http://www.citizensadvice.org.uk/rooting_out_the_rogues.pdf.

Cornwell J., Levenson, R., Sonola, L. and Poteliakhoff, E. (2012) *Continuity of Care for Older Hospital Patients. A Call for Action*. London: The King's Fund, available at: http://www.kingsfund.org.uk/publications/continuity-care-older-hospital-patients.

Department for Work and Pensions (2006) *Security in Retirement: Towards A New Pensions System*. White Paper, Cm 6841, available at: http://www.dwp.gov.uk/docs/white-paper-complete.pdf.

Department of Health (2002) *National Service Framework for Older People: Interim Report on Age Discrimination*. London: Department of Health.

Duncan, C. and Loretto, W. (2004) 'Never the right age? Gender and age based discrimination in employment' *Gender, Work and Organisation* 11(1), 95–115.

EIRO (2008) *Counting the Cost: Working Conditions of Migrants*, available at: http://www.eurofound.europa.eu/pubdocs/2008/893/en/1/EF08893EN.pdf.

EIRO (2009) *Drawing on Experience – Older Women Workers in Europe*, available at: http://www.eurofound.europa.eu/publications/htmlfiles/ef0885.htm.

Ellinson, G. and Gunstone, B. (2009) *Sexual Orientation Explored: a Study of Identity, Attraction, Behaviour and Attitudes in 2009*. Manchester: Equality and Human Rights Commission.

Equality Authority, Ireland (2004) *Implementing Equality for Older People*, available at: http://www.equality.ie/Files/Implementing%20Equality%20for%20Older%20People.pdf.

Equality and Human Rights Commission (EHRC) (2011a) Code of Practice on Employment, available at http://www.equalityhumanrights.com/legal-and-policy/equality-act/equality-act-codes-of-practice/.

Equality and Human Rights Commission (EHRC) (2011b) Code of Practice on Equal Pay, available at http://www.equalityhumanrights.com/legal-and-policy/equality-act/equality-act-codes-of-practice/.

Equality and Human Rights Commission (EHRC) (2011c) *How Fair is Britain? Equality, Human Rights and Good Relations in 2010*, http://www.equalityhumanrights.com/uploaded_files/triennial_review/how_fair_is_britain_ch11.pdf.

European Commission (2004) *Employment in Europe 2004*, available at: http://europa.eu/legislation_summaries/employment_and_social_policy/situation_in_europe/c10137_en.htm.

European Commission (2007) Special Eurobarometer Survey 263 *Discrimination in the European Union*, available at: http://ec.europa.eu/public_opinion/archives/ebs/ebs_263_sum_en.pdf.

European Commission (2010) *Employment in Europe 2010*, available at: http://ec.europa.eu/social/main.jsp?catId=738&langId=en&pubId=593.

European Foundation for the Improvement of Living and Working Conditions (Eurofound) (2009) *Women Managers and Hierarchical Structures in Working Life*, available at: http://www.eurofound.europa.eu/pubdocs/2008/103/en/1/EF08103EN.pdf.

European Monitoring Centre on Racism and Xenophobia (2006) *Muslims in the European Union: Discrimination and Islamophobia*, available at: http://fra.europa.eu/fraWebsite/attachments/Manifestations_EN.pdf.

European Union Agency for Fundamental Rights (2010) *Handbook on European Non-Discrimination Law*, available at: http://www.echr.coe.int/NR/rdonlyres/DACA17B3–921E–4C7C-A2EE–3CDB68B0133E/0/ENG_FRA_CASE_LAW_HANDBOOK_01.pdf.

Eurostat (2011) Demography Report 2010, available at: http://bookshop.europa.eu/en/demography-report–2010-pbKEET10001/

Fontanella-Khan, J. (2012) 'EU pushes 40% quota for women on boards', *Financial Times* 3 September, available at: http://www.ft.com/cms/s/0/65f494e6-f5e7–11e1-a6c2–00144feabdc0.html#axzz28oHg4ziE.

Government Equalities Office (2010) 'Caste Discrimination and Harassment in Great Britain', Research Paper 2010/8, available at: http://www.homeoffice.gov.uk/publications/equalities/research/caste-discrimination/caste-discrimination-summary?view=Binary.

Government Equalities Office (2012) 'Equal civil marriage: a consultation', available at: http://www.homeoffice.gov.uk/publications/about-us/consultations/equal-civil-marriage/consultation-document?view=Binary.

Hannett, S. (2003) 'Equality at the intersections: the legislative and judicial failure to tackle multiple discrimination' *Oxford Journal of Legal Studies* 23(1), 65–86.

Home Office (2000) 'Press for Change', *Report of the Interdepartmental Working Group On Transsexual People*, available at: http://www.pfc.org.uk/files/workgrp/wgtrans.pdf.

Home Office (2011) *Racist Incidents, England and Wales 2010/11*, available at: http://www.homeoffice.gov.uk/publications/science-research-statistics/research-statistics/crime-research/hosf0111/.

International Labour Organization (ILO) (2004) 'Towards a fair deal for migrant workers in the global economy'. International Labour Conference, 92nd Session, Geneva: International Labour Office, available at: http://www.ilo.org/public/english/standards/relm/ilc/ilc92/pdf/rep-vi.pdf.

Knauer, N. (2009) 'LGBT elder law: toward equity in aging' *Harvard Journal of Law and Gender* 32(1), 1–58.

Kochman, A. (1997) 'Gay and lesbian elderly: historical overview and implications for social work practice' *Journal of Gay and Lesbian Social Services* 6(1), 1–9.

McGregor, J. (2002) 'Stereotypes and older workers' *Journal of Social Policy New Zealand* 18, 163–77.

McKay, S. and Middleton, S. (1998) *Characteristics of Older Workers: Secondary Analysis of the Family and Working Lives Survey*, Research Reports RR4 and RR45, Centre for Research in Social Policy, Loughborough University. Department for Education and Employment.

McKay, S., Craw, M. and Chopra, D. (2006) *Migrant Workers in England and Wales: An Assessment of Migrant Worker Health and Safety Risks*. London: Health and Safety Executive.

Metcalfe, H. (1990) *Older Workers: Employers' Attitudes and Practices*. Institute of Manpower Studies.

MetLife Mature Market Institute (2006) *Out and Aging: The MetLife Study of Lesbian and Gay Baby Boomers*, November 2006. Westport: MetLife Mature Market Institute, available at: http://www.lgbtagingcenter.org/resources/resource.cfm?r=31.

Miller, M., André, A., Ebin, J. and Bessonova, L. (2007) 'Bisexual Health'. National Gay and Lesbian Taskforce, available at: http://www.thetaskforce.org/reports_and_research/bisexual_health.

Mitchell, M., Howarth, C., Kotecha, M. and Creegan, C. (2009) *Sexual Orientation Research Review 2008*. London: Equality and Human Rights Commission.

O'Brien, K.S., Latner, J.D., Ebneter, D. and Hunter, J.A. (2012) 'Obesity discrimination: the role of physical appearance, personal ideology, and anti-fat prejudice' *International Journal of Obesity*, available at: http://www.ncbi.nlm.nih.gov/pubmed/22531085.

Office for National Statistics (2004) *Focus on Older People*, available at: http://collections.europarchive.org/tna/20040722124833/statistics.gov.uk/focuson/olderpeople/.

Pensions Commission (2004) *Pensions: Challenges and Choices*. HMSO.

River, L. (2006) *A Feasibility Study of the Needs of Older Lesbians in Camden and Surrounding Boroughs*. Report to Age Concern Camden, available at: www.polari.org.

Rodgers, G. and Rodgers, J. (1989) *Precarious Jobs in Labour Market Regulation: The Growth of Atypical Employment in Western Europe*, Brussels: International Institute for Labour Studies and Free University of Brussels.

Rubin, J., Rendall, M.S., Rabinovich, L., Tsang, F., Janta, B. and Van Oranje-Nassau, C. (2008) 'Migrant women in the EU labour force' *Rand Europe*, available at: http://www.rand.org/pubs/technical_reports/2008/RAND_TR591.3.pdf.

Sandberg, R. and Doe, N. (2007) 'Religious exemptions in discrimination law' *Cambridge Law Journal* 66(2), 302–12.

San Francisco Human Rights Commission and Aging and Adult Services Commission (2003) *Aging in the Lesbian Gay Bisexual Transgender Communities*, available at: http://sf-hrc.org/modules/showdocument.aspx?documentid=1797.

Sargeant, M. (ed) (2008) *The Law on Age Discrimination in the EU*. Alphen aan den Rijn: Kluwer Law International.

Sargeant, M. (2009a) 'Age discrimination, redundancy payments and length of service' *Modern Law Review* 72(4), 628–34.

Sargeant, M. (2009b) 'Gender and the Pensions Acts 2007–2008' *Industrial Law Journal* 38, 143–48.

Sargeant, M. (2011a) *Age Discrimination: Ageism in Employment and Service Provision*. Farnham: Gower Publishing.

Sargeant, M. (2011b) 'The European Court of Justice and age discrimination' *Journal of Business Law* 2, 144–59.

Spencer, S. (2008) *Equality and Diversity in Jobs and Services: City Policies for Migrants in Europe*, EIRO, available at: http://www.eurofound.europa.eu/pubdocs/2008/71/en/3/EF0871EN.pdf.

Sweiry, D. and Willits, M. (2012) *Attitudes to Age in Britain 2010/11*, available at: http://research.dwp.gov.uk/asd/asd5/ih2011–2012/ihr7.pdf.

Taylor, P. and Walker, A. (1994) 'The ageing workforce: employers' attitudes towards older people', *Work, Employment and Society* 8(4), 569–91.

TUC (2008) *Hard Work, Hidden Lives: the Short Report of the Commission on Vulnerable Employment*. London: TUC.

United Nations Department of Economic and Social Affairs Population Division (2002) *World Population Ageing: 1950–2050*, available at: http://www.un.org/esa/population/publications/worldageing19502050/.

United Nations (2009) *Follow-up to the Second World Assembly on Ageing; Report of the Secretary-General*, July, available at: http://social.un.org/index/Ageing/Resources/UNReportsandResolutions/GeneralAssemblyReports.aspx.

Vulnerable Worker Enforcement Forum (2008) *Final Report and Government Conclusions August*. Department for Business, Enterprise and Regulatory Reform, available at: http://www.berr.gov.uk/files/file47317.pdf.

Ward, R., Jones, R., Hughes, J., Humberstone, N. and Pearson, R. (2008) 'Intersections of Ageing and Sexuality', Chapter 4 in Richard Ward and Bill Bytheway (eds), *Researching Age and Multiple Discrimination*. London: Centre for Policy on Ageing.

Whittle, S., Turner, L. and Al-Alami, M. (2007) *Engendered Penalties: Transgender and Transsexual People's Experiences of Inequality and Discrimination*. London: The Equalities Review.

Index